D0443183

HOW TO WORK
MIRACLES
IN YOUR LIFE

The Golden Secret of
Successful Living

HOW TO WORK MIRACLES IN YOUR LIFE

The Golden Secret of Successful Living

Wm. S. Casselberry, Ph.D.

West Nyack, N.Y.

PARKER PUBLISHING COMPANY, INC.

© 1964 BY

WM. S. CASSELBERRY

ALL RIGHTS RESERVED. NO PART OF THIS BOOK
MAY BE REPRODUCED IN ANY FORM, BY MIM-
EOGRAPH OR ANY OTHER MEANS, WITHOUT
PERMISSION IN WRITING FROM THE PUBLISHER.

LIBRARY OF CONGRESS
CATALOG CARD NUMBER: 64–24020

Second printing .... June, 1965

PRINTED IN THE UNITED STATES OF AMERICA
44149—B&P

By the same Author:

How To Use Psychology In Everyday Living

To My Wife

ALTA

With grateful appreciation for
her help, and for her patience
while I neglected her during
the writing of this book.

A BIRD'S EYE VIEW OF THE CONTENTS

In Chapter 1 you learn what you must do to get the most out of life. You acquire the Three Golden Keys to miraculous power.

To get what you want out of life you must make only wise decisions.

In Chapter 2 you learn the complete Decision-Making Technique and how to use it.

Chapter 3 gives you 11 special procedures to help you make only wise decisions.

In Chapter 4 you learn how to make yourself do what you know you *should* do. You also learn how to keep yourself from doing what you know you should *not* do.

Chapter 5 shows you how to establish all the good, new habits you need to get the most out of life. You also learn how to stop any old habits which keep you away from the good things of life.

In Chapter 6 you learn the important facts about you and your physical make-up. You lay the foundation for the creation of the physical energy you need to get the most out of life.

In Chapter 7 you learn the Five-Step Plan for the improvement of your physical condition. You learn how to get the extra physical power you need to get the most out of life. You also learn how to keep yourself out of physical trouble.

Chapter 8 shows you how to use your spare time to develop more power and get the most out of life.

In Chapter 9 you learn how to make more money, to conserve your money, and to use it wisely.

Chapter 10 gives you the Golden Secret. It shows you how to

use the contents of this book. It shows you how, as you journey through life, to get the good things you want.

The Suggestion

Would you like a more detailed description of the subject matter? If so, read the Table of Contents. If not, go to Chapter 1.

CONTENTS

Use the Keys all together. This too will help you get the most from life.

Seven Procedures to avoid stimulus-response arcs. (Seven ways to keep yourself from doing something.) Eliminate the signals, stop your visualized images, stop your inner speech, stop your implicit muscle movements which start the wrong arcs. Remove or minimize the pleasure which comes with the act. Increase the pain. Think about the bad consequences of the act. Improve your physical condition. To avoid an act use all the Procedures at the same time. The suggestion. Instructions if you have not yet learned the 18 Steps of the Decision-Making Technique.

and your cells. You can eat or drink harmful materials. Harmful materials in your lungs. Harmful materials through your skin. How you are punished if you allow harmful materials to reach your cells. *Waste products in your blood.* How the waste products are produced. How you can increase the waste materials in your blood. How you are punished if you allow the waste products to accumulate. *The starvation of your cells.* How you can starve your cells. How you are punished if you don't supply your cells with enough protein. How you are punished if you don't ingest enough carbohydrate food. How you are punished if you fail to supply your cells with enough of the unsaturated fatty acids. How you are punished if you don't supply your cells with enough vitamins, and in the right balance. Vitamins A, B_1, B_2, niacin, C, D, E. The vitamins work together. How you are punished if you fail to supply your cells with enough of the right minerals. Calcium and phosphorus. Iron. Iodine. Oxygen. Water. *Failure to eat the right food.* How you can eat the wrong foods. White flour foods are wrong for you. Sugar and sugar foods are wrong for you. Foods stored for long periods are wrong for you. Foods grown on poor soil are wrong for you. How you are punished if you don't eat the right foods. The development of a germ disease. It's like a battle. How you are punished by infections. How do you react? *Too much stress.* How you are punished if you experience too much stress. Three ways you can bring illness upon yourself. The most popular way to become ill. You can choose your illness. *How you are rewarded if you take good care of your cells.* The secret of proper care of your cells. You have two choices. The suggestion.

7. Turn On Your Physical Power • 141

How to get more power. If you are now in physical trouble. What to do if you are well. *The Five-Step Plan to increase your physical power to get the most out of life.* A. Protect your cells from physical damage. B. Keep poisons and harmful materials out of yourself and away from your cells. C. Keep the waste materials inside you to a minimum and remove them as they form. Three priceless rules. Relax. Sleep well! Exercise. Maintain a good posture. Keep your elimination normal. Breathe deeply and get plenty of fresh air into your lungs. Drink enough water. *D.* Supply your cells with their complete nourishment. Eat the right foods for you. Make a list of the foods you eat. Remove certain foods from your list. The foods you should remove. Add to your list the foods you should eat. The foods you should add. Can you secure the right foods? Chew your food. Separate the high starches and the high proteins. Don't overeat. Eat simply. Add the supplements you need. *E.* Keep your stress to a minimum. The final reminder. Use the Decision-Making Technique and make your wise decision. What to do if you decided against the plan. What to do if you decided in favor of the plan. What will you do with your extra energy? The suggestion.

HOW TO WORK
MIRACLES
IN YOUR LIFE

**The Golden Secret of
Successful Living**

Chapter 1

HOW TO GET THE MOST OUT OF LIFE

*In this chapter you learn what you must
do to get the most out of life. You acquire the Three Golden Keys.*

To get what you want from life, to get rid of your present
troubles and problems and to avoid mistakes in the future,
your best procedure is to use:
The Three Golden Keys
1. Make only wise decisions.
2. Build the necessary good habits and eliminate your bad
habits.
3. Develop excellent health.
There are only three Golden Keys. But with these three keys
you can unlock all the doors to all the good things of life.

Is this too much to ask?

Now you may say, "Certainly, if a person always makes wise
decisions, if he sets up all the good habits he needs, if he gets
rid of all his bad habits and then if he always has excellent
health, he can accomplish just about anything. But how is he
going to learn to make only wise decisions? How is he to build
all the good habits? How can he break all his bad habits? How
can he develop excellent health? How can he keep from making mistakes? I've tried many times, but I never could do it."

1

Actually, it isn't nearly as difficult as it might seem. All you need is (1) an understanding of the basic principles and (2) the right methods. These you get in this book.

Then (3) you need some spare time.

That's where *you* come in.

Spare time is time you have left over after you do everything you *must* do, or which you feel you must do.

In this spare time you can learn to use the Three Golden Keys.

Right now you undoubtedly have *some* spare time. If you wish, you can begin the use of the Three Golden Keys almost at once.

But you are not limited to your present spare time. Because of mechanization and automation, the modern trend is toward more and more spare time for everyone. You should have much more spare time in the future. What better way can you find to use your present and future spare time than to master the Three Golden Keys and get the most out of life?

Our program

1. We shall start with the Decision-Making Technique. This comes first because everything you do starts with a decision. If your steps toward the good things of life are to be in the right direction, they must be directed by wise decisions.

To get the good things of life, which you don't have now, you must make wise decisions.

To eliminate your present troubles and problems you must make wise decisions.

To avoid trouble in the future you must make only wise decisions.

2. Then we shall consider your habits.

To get the good things of life you must have the right habits.

To eliminate your present troubles and problems you may have to develop some good habits and you may have to stop certain bad habits.

To avoid trouble in the future you must develop the right habits.

3. Third, we shall see just what you must do to have good health.

To get the good things of life you must have good health and plenty of energy.

To eliminate your present troubles and problems you need health and energy.

To avoid troubles and problems in the future you must have good health and an abundance of energy.

4. We shall see how you can take some of your spare time, use the Three Golden Keys, and get the most out of life.

5. Finally, by way of illustration, you will learn how to use the Three Golden Keys to get one of the good things of life— money. You will learn how to increase your income and how to handle your money wisely.

Why we start with wise decisions

Suppose you have not yet found your right vocation. Think how quickly you can get into the right vocation if all your decisions are wise.

Imagine how rapidly you can advance in your vocation or profession if every decision you make is exactly right.

Are you unmarried? Would you like to be married? Do you think you would find your right marriage partner more quickly if you make only wise decisions?

Are you married? Do you see how you can improve your marriage adjustment if you make only wise decisions?

Are you a parent? If you make only wise decisions, and you act on them, your children will be well-trained and jewels in your crown.

If you make only wise decisions, think how much you can add to your health!

Suppose you are interested in some special activity. It might be that of student, athlete, or entertainer. You might be interested in some recreational activity. Can you see how much faster you will advance if you always make wise decisions?

You must deal with people. Think how much more popular and well-liked you will be when all your human-relation decisions are right. Think how much happier you will be at home. Think of the prestige and personal influence you will enjoy!

Do you have a small amount of money to invest? If all your decisions are correct, every investment yields a good return. You will become wealthy.

Wise decisions bring big rewards

Look back over your life. How much better off would you be, right now, if you had not made some of your bad decisions of the past? Think how much better off you will be in the future if you make only half of the bad decisions you would otherwise make! But you don't have to stop with such a small improvement. Think what your life will be like if you *never again* make a bad decision!

From the above discussion, the importance of wise decisions should be clear.

Also, from the above discussion, it should be clear that to get the most out of life, soonest and easiest, you should first learn to make wise decisions.

The suggestion

Now read Chapter 2. Learn how to make wise decisions.

Chapter 2

YOUR MOST POWERFUL TOOL FOR GETTING WHAT YOU WANT OUT OF LIFE

In this chapter you investigate the decision-making process. You learn the complete Decision-Making Technique and how to use it.

Agassiz was a famous naturalist, geologist, and teacher.

The story is told that one day a new pupil came to him for training. Agassiz gave the young man a fish and these instructions: "Take this fish. Study it for a day. Then come back and tell me what you discover."

The young man studied the fish and reported. Agassiz told him, "Go back and study the fish again. Study it for three days and tell me all you learn about the fish."

What is the point of the story? The point is that you can take a quick look at something and learn a few things about it. You can study it more and learn more. The more you study it and the more you think about it, the more you see in it and the more you learn about it.

Now the assignment is not to study a fish. The assignment is to study the mechanics of a decision.

We study the decision-making process for an hour

This is what we find in an hour's study:

When you make a decision you contemplate a possible action. Then you say words to yourself. You say, "I'll do it," or "I'll not do it."

At the same time you say the words, something happens inside you. A physical set, or tendency, develops. You get set to act in the direction of your words.

When you have both the words and the right set, you make a decision.

Do you say to yourself, "I shall go to bed right now"? With these words do you feel a definite inclination to act out the plan and go to bed? If so, you make a decision.

On the other hand, suppose you say the words, "I'll do it," or "I'll not do it." But you don't have the right set. Then you don't make a decision.

Perhaps you say to yourself, "I shall go to bed right now." But you are set to stay up and watch TV. Then you have not made a decision. You have just said some words to yourself.

You have often heard of people who, under pressure, say, "I'll never touch another drop of liquor." But their set—their muscular alignment, their physical inclination, their plan—is to take a drink as soon as they can. Then they haven't made a decision at all. They have just pronounced some empty words.

To make a decision (1) you must say words to yourself. These words state that you have chosen or rejected a certain line of action. (2) Along with the words must come a positive set to act as stated by your words.

We study the decision-making process for a day

We have studied the decision-making process for an hour. Above is our report.

Were Agassiz here, supervising our research, he might say, "Very good for a start. Now study the decision-making process for a day and tell me what you discover."

This is what we learn:

1. When you make a decision you start with a suggested course of action. This we call a "plan."

2. The plan always has a goal. The goal of the plan is to provide certain benefits.

Suppose the plan is to invest in a business. If successful, the investment offers a return of 20 percent on your investment. This return is the goal of the plan.

3. A plan always has some disadvantages. The disadvantages usually lie in the amount of money, time, effort, or inconvenience necessary to carry out the plan.

4. When you finally start to make your decision, you may use a well-known method. You may weigh the possible rewards and benefits of the plan against the possible disadvantages, trouble, and cost. If you think the advantages are greater, you accept the plan. If you think the *dis*advantages are greater, you reject the plan.

Above is the report of our findings when we study the decision-making process for a day. Again Agassiz might say, "Quite satisfactory for a short study. Now study the decision-making procedure for a week."

What we learn in a week

1. We see the plan, just as we did before.

Now we also see that we must always know the facts about the plan.

The more complicated the plan, the more important it is to get all the vital facts about it. But also, the more complicated the plan, the more difficult it is to get all the important facts.

Whether complicated or simple, however, we must have all the facts about the plan.

Suppose, for example, that you are invited to go on a tour.

That's the proposed plan. The cost will be $350 which will pay all expenses for a month's tour of Mexico. It sounds like a fine idea. You decide to go.

When you get to Mexico you discover that you are to travel on the ordinary Mexican public buses which run from town to town. It's picturesque. But also it is crowded. It's uncomfortable. You must share the bus with farmers, produce, and chickens.

You resolve, in the future, to get all the facts about any proposed plan.

2. The plan is always suggested by a situation.

A plan is a proposed line of action. You can't have an action without something to start it; you can't have a plan without a situation to suggest it. You never sit down and say, "Not having anything to accomplish, I shall now set up a few plans."

Why is the situation so important? Because you only consider a plan when you want to produce a benefit, either for yourself or for someone else. To produce a benefit the plan must fit the situation.

Suppose, as an example, that a lady friend is about to have a birthday. Unknown to you, the friend is allergic to cats. That's the situation.

You think you will give your friend a cat as a birthday present.

It is obvious that the plan doesn't fit the situation.

To be sure the plan fits the situation, you must always get the important facts about the situation.

3. Although the situation suggests the plan, it suggests it in only a vague way. Someone must develop the plan.

One possibility is that *you* consider the situation, and *you* develop the plan. Your car may break down, for example, and you think of a plan to get it going again.

The other possibility is that someone else looks at the situation and *he* develops the plan.

A salesman may develop the plan. He may ask you to buy a

house, a typewriter, or a new type of lipstick. A relative may think of the plan—that he visit you at a certain time. A friend may offer a plan. He may say, "Let's see a show tonight."

Millions of plans are proposed by ads. "Come to Kozy Kottages this summer," "Buy Hurrah, the new mouth wash," "Trade in your old car on this beautiful Brownmobile," "Smoke Gaspers, the *mild* cigarette!"

4. The reward of a successful plan can be almost any good thing you can name. It can be money, power, prestige, personal satisfaction, health, a new skill, love, marriage, travel, success, knowledge, popularity, personal achievement, security, relaxation, or service to others.

5. The possible loss from some plans can be very great.

Perhaps you contemplate investing a large sum of money. There is the possibility that, if the plan should fail, you will lose all your money.

You look at another plan. The plan is to shoot the rapids of the Colorado River in a canoe. A glance at the plan shows you that the penalty for failure could be the loss of your life.

6. The penalties may appear during the operation of the plan or after the plan is completed.

Suppose you take an ocean trip and get seasick. The disadvantage comes during the trip.

When you get home you may be so tired you wish you hadn't taken the trip. In this case the disadvantage appears after the plan is executed.

We study the process for a month

Agassiz, of course, wouldn't be satisfied with only a week's study. So we study the decision-making process for a month. This is what we learn:

1. A decision can be small, medium, or big.

2. A small or unimportant decision is one from which you can lose but little if the decision is wrong. Also, you can gain little if your decision is right.

Nothing much depends on a small decision—not much money, time, reputation, safety, or peace of mind.

Examples of small decisions are these: You decide to see a movie, to play a game of golf, to read the newspaper, to take a short walk, or to call on a friend.

You make many such small decisions every day.

3. We see, also, that a decision can be of medium importance.

A decision of medium importance is one from which you can lose considerable if the decision is wrong. The rewards are reasonably large if the plan is successful.

Here are some examples of medium-sized decisions: You decide to buy a movie camera and projector, to buy a color TV, to join a local country club, to subscribe to a newspaper for a year, to take a 50-mile hike, to take up a course of study with a professional.

You make many decisions of medium importance.

4. An important decision is one from which you can lose a great deal if you make a poor decision. Or you can gain tremendously if you make a wise decision.

You are faced with many important decisions. For example: Should you get married? Should you enlist in one of the armed services? Should you go to college? Should you seek a career on the stage? Should you have an operation? Should you get a divorce? Should you quit your job and try to get a better one? Should you sue someone? Should you buy a certain business? Should you have treatments by a psychiatrist? Should you accept a position in a foreign country? Should you change your religion? Should you put all your money into stocks?

When you make an important decision you have much to gain from a wise decision. You also can lose much if you make an unwise decision.

Are you an executive in a large corporation? Do you own your own business? Are you a prominent politician? Are you a general, admiral, lawyer, judge, physician, or surgeon? If so you may make many very important decisions every day. Why are all these decisions so important? Because another person, your organization, or your counrty has much to lose if you make an unwise decision. There is also much to gain if you make a wise decision.

5. In our month's study we learn that you must make decisions, not in just one field, but in many different fields. You must jump from one field to another.

Today, possibly, you must decide whether or not to buy a new car. Tomorrow you must decide whether or not to accept a new job. Next you must decide if you should talk with the school people about Junior and his school grades. Following this you must decide whether or not to lend a friend $500.

Here are other common decisions in many different fields: Should you go on the hunting trip this year? Should you learn to play golf? Should you buy a certain property? Should you make a real attempt to keep relatives from interfering in your home life? Should you sue the neighbor who built his garage one foot over onto your property? Should the teen-aged daughter be allowed to wear high heels? Should you run for a city office? Should you change your dentist? Should you learn to play duplicate bridge? Should you go on a reducing diet?

These are the kinds of decisions you *must* make. They come in many different fields. You must make these decisions in response to the urging of the people around you, in response to changes in the people and things in your environment, and in answer to the demands of your physical condition.

6. We have seen that a plan always has a goal. When you accept the plan you accept the goal.

What makes it complicated is this: Sometimes a plan has two goals. If you don't consider both goals, you may make an unwise decision.

A business acquaintance, for example, recommends a certain

specialty shop. The announced goal of his plan is to enable you to buy interesting specialties at a fair price. The undisclosed goal is to enable him to earn a commission.

Suppose a friend suggests that you join a social group which meets every Thursday evening. The group meets, you are told, for social enjoyment and the study of current events. Those are the announced goals.

You go once as a visitor. Everyone makes a fuss over you. You enjoy yourself immensely. You like the discussion of current events. You think it's a fine group.

You know that if you join the group you accept the plan. You also accept the goal of the plan. In this case, would you join the group without determining the real goal of the plan? You should not. Suppose the real goal is to instruct the members of the group in the ways of Communism. If you don't know this real goal of the plan, you might join the group and be sorry ever after.

7. We learn that you should check the goal of a plan against your personal goals.

You could check the goal of a plan against your likes and dislikes, of course. But this is a poor way to judge a goal. The reason is that your likes and dislikes change. Sometimes they change rapidly. Also, it's better to be governed by reason than by your emotions.

The best way to judge the goal of a plan is to check it against your personal goals. If the goal of the plan harmonizes with your personal goals, you may wish to decide for the plan.

As an example let us say that one of your personal goals is to learn to play golf well. Now a friend suggests a plan. The plan is that you join him and take a series of golf lessons with a pro. The goal of the plan is to improve your ability to play golf. The goal of the plan harmonizes with your personal goal. The plan passes this test.

But suppose another plan is suggested. The goal of this plan is to learn to dance. This goal doesn't harmonize with your personal goal, which is to play a good game of golf. You may refuse to follow the plan.

To judge the goal of any plan, compare the goal with your personal goals. Would you like to be able to make this comparison almost instantly? It's easy. All you have to do is write out all your personal goals. Then memorize them, and you will have them for ready reference. There is more about this in Chapter 3.

8. You can't study the decision-making process without realizing this: You must have sufficient knowledge in the field of the plan.

To make a wise decision you must know and understand the plan. To understand the plan you must have sufficient facts in the general field of the plan.

Suppose a friend asks you to invest some money in a new company. The company is going to extract runkles from velderfloss. Wouldn't you say, "The plan may be good, but how can I tell? I don't know anything at all about either runkles or velderfloss. For all I know, there may be no such thing as a runkle. I can't judge the plan. I don't have any facts in the general field of runkle extraction."

Do you plan to buy a lot and to sell it at a profit? If you do, you will need the general facts in the field of real estate investments.

Are you about to select a plan for training children? Then you should have the facts in the general field of child psychology.

Must you judge a proposed plan to make self-developing pictures? If so, you should have the facts in the general field of chemistry and photography.

When you think about accepting a plan, you must be sure you have enough knowledge in the general field of the plan. If you don't, you should either (1) postpone the decision until you can get the facts you need, (2) decide against the plan or (3) secure the services of someone who knows the facts in the field and who can explain them to you.

9. Usually, when you decide on a plan, *you* execute the plan or you have much to do with it.

When you decide to hike in the mountains, *you* take the hike.

If you decide on a plan to sell air conditioners, *you* sell them.

If you decide on a plan to sue a man, *you* sue him. True enough, your lawyer will do the legal work. But you will have to do some work with him. Also you must supply the money.

Are you about to decide in favor of a plan? You must have the physical strength and endurance to put the plan through.

10. Our study shows that your physical habits must also be right for any plan you accept.

There are two kinds of physical habits.

First, you have a set of physical movements which you use over and over. These are the way you move, stand, and sit. They are the way you gesture, wrinkle your brow, and the way you smile. These habits include your grace or awkwardness, your speed of movement, and your eye-hand coordination.

Does a plan call for certain basic physical movements? If so, be sure you have the needed "movement" habits before you decide to accept the plan.

Suppose you always move fast, you talk loudly, and you are always in a hurry. Then a proposed plan to act as usher at funerals would not fit your physical habits. Are you slow-moving and with poor eye-hand coordination? Then a decision to become a juggler would be unwise.

Second, you combine or include your basic physical movements with certain activities. This produces your working habits, your play habits, and your skills. Among these habits and skills you find such activities as driving a car, bowling, operating a typewriter, riding a bicycle, reading, writing, speaking in public, and carrying on conversations.

Does the plan call for certain physical habits or skills? If so, to accept the plan, you must have, or develop, the right habits and skills. Only then will your decision to follow the plan be wise.

11. You must also have the right physical *qualifications* for the proposed plan. These are such items as your height, weight, strength, endurance, appearance, volume, and quality of voice.

12. As we study the decision-making process we see that it is important to have sufficient control of any plan you accept.

Sometimes you must have *complete* control of the plan. Sometimes you can give up some of your control. The rule is this: You must always have *sufficient* control.

Suppose you are asked to supply all the capital for a new company. The company will manufacture a much-needed product. You learn that there will be a president and a general manager who will operate the company. You will be a stockholder. Since you will not have control of the business you are suspicious of the plan. Why? Because your money will be in the business, but your money will be controlled entirely by others. If they bungle and begin to fail you can't do anything about it. You would just have to watch your money disappear.

Does this mean that you must decide against every plan over which you don't have complete control? No. There are many times when, to accept a plan, you must give up much of your control.

When you go on a conducted tour, which may be a very fine thing to do, you give up much control. You do the same when you ride on a plane, train, or boat. Also when you marry you give up much control of your affairs.

Sometimes it is absolutely necessary to have complete control.

In other cases you can delegate some of your control and still carry out your plan.

How much control you must have depends on the situation. But you must always have *enough* control.

13. The sort of thinking habits you have are important in decision-making. You need the right thinking habits to go with any plan you accept.

Your thinking habits include the way you think—fast or slowly, accurately or inaccurately, logically or illogically, clearly or unclearly.

Suppose a proposed plan requires accurate thinking. You think inaccurately. You tend to get the facts mixed. Then your thinking habits aren't right for the plan. If you decide to accept the plan you may make a big mistake. You may fail completely when you try to execute the plan.

On the other hand, the proposed plan may require slow and accurate thinking. If this is your habitual way of thinking, well and good. To this extent your thinking habits are right for this plan.

What you think about most of the time is also part of your thinking habits. If you think most of the time about bowling or cooking, a proposed plan to sell life insurance wouldn't fit the thinking habits. But a plan to sell bowling or cooking equipment might be acceptable.

14. Your emotional habits have much to do with the way you carry out any plan you accept.

Your emotions influence your actions. They grease the wheels, as it were. Or they put on the brakes.

What happens if your emotions aren't right for the plan? You may find it difficult, or impossible, to work along the lines of the plan.

Suppose the suggested plan is to become a salesman. Assume that your emotional habits are described by the words worry, anxiety, and fear. Then your emotional habits aren't right for the plan—for selling. Or we could say that the activities normally carried on by a salesman do not fit your emotional habits. You would not be able to work as a salesman. You couldn't carry out the plan.

But if you have the emotional habits of hope, optimism, and courage, that's different. Now you have some of the right emotional habits needed for the plan to sell a product or service.

15. Your physical habits are important. Your physical habits include your "when" habits and your skills.

Suppose you use your reading and writing habits as a clerk. Your "when" habit is to use these clerical habits between 9 and 5, five days a week. A proposed plan to use these work habits in the evening or on Saturday would not fit your "when" habit.

If you accept a proposed plan, your basic habits and your "when" habits must be right for the plan.

You can change your "when" habits, of course, just as you can change any habit (Chapters 4 and 5). But as long as you have the habit you must take it into account when you consider a plan.

Your skills, too, are physical habits. Skill in speaking a foreign language or in playing bridge is a physical habit. True enough, considerable mental activity may go with both of these skills. But the actual performance is a physical habit.

When you think about accepting a plan, you must consider your physical habits, your skills, and your "when" habits.

16. When you make a decision you must consider your environment.

Your environment is everything around you which affects you in any way.

Around you are certain people, pets, rooms, a street, and a neighborhood. These are all part of your environment.

At your place of work there are certain people, rooms, offices, furniture, equipment, and a place to eat and rest. These are also part of your environment.

You have certain possessions which are part of your environment. These include your furniture, equipment, Hi Fi, TV, cars, and possibly a boat or a bicycle.

There is your capital—money in the bank, stocks, bonds, and mortgages.

Finally come your obligations and debts.

All of these are parts of your environment. Your environment consists of everything around you which affects you in any way.

Our study of the decision-making process shows that your environment must be taken into account when you consider a plan.

Suppose the proposed plan is to take a trip to Europe. The plan would require $2500. You have only $2000. Your environment isn't right for the plan.

Now suppose you change the plan. Now it's to take a different trip. You are to pay $2000 down and $1000 in twelve monthly installments when you return from the trip. You look at your monthly obligations. You see that your obligations and living expenses now equal your total income. Your environment isn't right for this new plan either. You can't pay the monthly installments.

If your environment isn't right for a suggested plan you may have to reject the plan.

17. When we study the decision-making process we see that you can't always be sure a plan will take you to a desired goal.

But we also see that you can make a shrewd guess. You can figure the odds.

By "odds" is meant the chances of one outcome appearing rather than another.

Is your proposed plan to toss a coin and have it come to rest heads up? The odds for success and failure are even. This is because there are only two possibilities. When you toss the coin it comes to rest with either heads or tails up.

Suppose you roll a regular six-sided die, as used in the game of dice. You have one chance in six of throwing a four. This is because any one of the six sides can come up, but only one side shows a four. Is your plan to roll a four in one throw? The odds are six to one against the success of your plan.

Suppose you think about placing a dollar on number 32 on the roulette table. You see that with 36 numbers, together with the 0 and 00 for the house, the odds are 38 to 1 against a win.

Usually it's quite easy to figure the odds when you can do it mathematically. But this isn't always possible. Sometimes you must make an educated guess. When this is true, your experience, education, and your general knowledge of the field come to your rescue.

Suppose you contemplate driving on a busy superhighway at the traffic peak. You are a good driver with much experience. You know all about the highway and its traffic. You wonder what the odds are for your safe arrival at your destination. You consider all the facts. You can't figure the odds mathematically. But as a guess you may decide that the odds are about 100 to 1 in favor of a safe trip.

Suppose, however, that you are driving a worn-out, ten-year-old car. You are tired and sleepy. Then you might figure the odds to be 2 to 1 in favor of an accident.

18. After a plan is accepted and executed, there are often repercussions. Somebody, or some group, organization, or country doesn't like the plan. Sometimes the reaction is so violent that the plan has to be changed or withdrawn.

Nobody wants to be embarrassed or inconvenienced. Nobody likes to be forced to change or withdraw his plan.

To avoid this, the customary procedure is to guess what the other fellow will do when you put a plan into effect.

Who is the "other fellow"? He is any other person involved in the plan, either directly or indirectly.

You might decide, for instance, to move your fence over two feet. Your neighbor might object to the plan—especially if your plan puts the fence on his lot. Your neighbor is the "other fellow."

In many cases there are people who are entitled to share in the decision. This is because they must help you carry out the plan. These people are the "other fellows." You see at once that you should consult these people, or take them into your confidence, before you make your decision.

Let us say that you are about to spend considerable money, or invest some funds. The money belongs to you and your spouse jointly. Before you make your final decision, take the matter up with your spouse. Your spouse is the "other fellow." Reach an agreement. If you don't, you may find yourself in trouble.

Many an executive has learned this the hard way. After learning, what does he do when he contemplates an important decision which affects the employees? He tests their reaction to the plan before he decides on the plan. The employees are the "other fellows."

A school principal used this plan effectively. Whenever he contemplated a new plan which involved the teachers, he first took it up in a general teachers' meeting. Every teacher had a chance to air his views. When everyone had spoken, the principal closed the meeting and made his decision. He made the decision and took the responsibility. If some of the teachers didn't like his decision, they accepted it philosophically. They realized that they all had had a chance to express their opinions. They knew also that the principal made his decision *after* he got the views of everyone affected.

You can use this procedure to advantage whenever you make decisions which affect others. Learn or guess the possible reactions of the other fellow. If you are a parent, use it with your children. Husbands should use it with their wives, wives with husbands, and executives with their employees. Learn or guess how the other fellow will react. Adjust your plan accordingly. Then the plan can be carried out much more easily.

19. In general, it is harder to determine what the other fellow will do (1) when you know little about the situation and the facts in the general field of the situation, (2) when you know little about the person's habits and guiding principles, and (3) when you know little about human nature.

Let's say that you are asked to sell a certain man a ticket to a charity affair by telephone. He is a complete stranger to you.

You know absolutely nothing about him. What will the man do when you ask for the money? From your knowledge of people you might make a guess. But you could be quite wrong. You don't have enough facts.

On the other hand, it is usually much easier to guess what the other person will do (1) when you know all about the situation and when you have plenty of facts in the general field, (2) when you are familiar with the person's habits and the principles which help guide him, and (3) when you know a lot about human nature.

As an example, can you guess how a member of your family will react if you present her with a fancy box of top-quality chocolates?

In many cases it is easy to learn how a person will react to a plan. Just ask him.

Mr. Green, for example, is about to leave for home late in the afternoon. He meets an old war buddy. His first thought is to take his friend home for dinner and to spend the night. But immediately his recollection of previous experiences flashes a warning light. "What," he thinks, "will the 'little woman' say? How will she react?" He telephones and finds out.

20. Sometimes several plans will take you to approximately the same goal. Usually one of the plans is best.

There is the young lieutenant in the army. He is in charge of a company for drill. He thinks of a good maneuver. That is his proposed plan. He gives the appropriate command. But almost before he finishes giving the command he thinks of a better plan to reach the same goal. Then he cancels the previous order and gives the new order for the execution of the new plan.

Theoretically, this could go on for a long time. The young officer might think of ten plans, each a little better than the previous plan.

Part of what the officer does is right. When he thinks of the first plan he should see if he can find a better plan. But he should find the better plan *before* he makes his decision and *before* he gives the command. When the young officer becomes an old officer, with years of experience, this is what he will always do. Does he contemplate an attack on the enemy's position? Possibly his staff suggests a plan. It is a good plan. But what other plans, he asks, will get the same or better results?

Always try to find the *best* plan.

21. You can make six different kinds of decisions.

You make a *tentative* decision when you accept a proposed plan with reservations. You have an understanding with yourself, and perhaps with others, that you may not, actually, act on the plan.

As an illustration, say a friend invites you to a reception next Friday evening. You would like to go. But another friend from out of town may arrive Friday afternoon. You decide to go to the reception provided your friend doesn't come until Saturday. This is a tentative decision.

You make a *firm* decision when you accept a proposed plan without reservations. You are set to carry out the plan.

Suppose you tell a real estate dealer that you will buy a certain property. You give him $1,000 as a deposit. You made a firm decision.

You make a *wise* decision when you use an efficient decision-making technique, and you use it correctly.

You make a *quick* decision when you accept or reject a plan immediately after it is suggested.

Someone asks, "Shall I file this survey?" At once you reply, "No. Throw it in the waste basket." That is a quick decision.

You make a *lasting* decision when you accept a plan and the decision is not changed. The plan is carried out.

You make a *snap* decision when you accept a proposed plan without thinking it through. It may turn out to be a good decision. It may not. It's a gamble.

Suppose someone says to you, "What are you going to do with the $10,000 you have in the bank? We're in an inflation economy. Why don't you put the money into some good real estate as a hedge against inflation?" You have given no thought to the matter. You know nothing about the field of real estate investment. If you reply at once, "That's a good idea. I'll do it," it's a snap decision.

Never make a snap decision. Snap decisions get you into trouble.

The only sort of decision you should ever make is a *wise* decision.

22. Desires and personal wants can exert a strong influence on your decisions. In fact, if you aren't careful, your desires will make your decisions for you and get you into all sorts of trouble.

Consider the young man in love. He has a strong desire to marry the girl. Why? Because she will make him a good wife? No. Because he *loves* her.

Love is a strong emotion. It brings about a great desire. Suppose the desire dominates. Then, the young man doesn't make the final decision at all. His *desire* makes the decision!

But the desire doesn't suffer if the decision is wrong. It is the young man who suffers!

The final decision must always be made with the careful use of a sound decision-making technique.

23. Before you make an important decision, you ponder. You weigh the evidence. You consider all the facts. You think about what you should do.

You know from your own experience that, in order to think clearly, two things are important. First, you must be in good physical condition. You must be *physically* fit to carry on your best *mental* activity.

For illustration, consider a man who is in extreme pain with a broken leg. Nobody would expect him to think clearly and to make important and wise decisions.

The worse your physical condition, the greater the likelihood that you will make bad decisions.

On the other hand, the better your physical condition the easier it is to think clearly.

Second, you must have the right surroundings.

Can you do intricate figuring in a noisy room with people phoning close by?

Can you study and learn easily while a radio commentator reports the news?

Can you think clearly when people close by are talking to each other and to you?

If you want to think clearly, you need to be undisturbed.

To free yourself from the strong influence of another person, you may have to get away from him.

To get away from the pressures of their normal surroundings, many people retire to a quiet place. They get completely away from all influences which might cause them to make a wrong decision. Then they think. They weigh all the factors and they consider all the facts.

It is reported that when he was finally ready to decide whether or not to run for Governor of Michigan, Mr. George Romney went off by himself for 24 hours. During this period he made his decision.

The final step

We have now reviewed the facts from our month's study of the decision-making process.

Were Agassiz here he would probably say, "So you think you have all the important facts? Very well. Now study the facts and draw your conclusions. See if you can establish a rule or law."

We act on his suggestion.

We see that we can sum up our facts in the form of a routine, or standard procedure. This gives us an established method. We can use it every time we wish to make a wise decision.

THE 18 STEP DECISION-MAKING TECHNIQUE

Step 1. Get all the important facts about the situation which suggested the plan.

Step 2. Gather the important facts about the proposed plan.

Step 3. Determine the goal of the plan.

Step 4. Check the goal of the proposed plan with your personal goals.

Step 5. Be sure you have enough general knowledge in the field of the plan.

Step 6. Be sure your physical condition and qualifications are right for the plan.

Step 7. Be sure you have enough control of the plan.

Step 8. Be sure you have the right thinking habits to enable you to carry out the proposed plan successfully.

Step 9. Be sure your emotional habits are right, to enable you to carry out the plan.

Step 10. Be sure your physical habits and skills are right for the plan.

Step 11. Your environment must be right for the proposed plan.

Step 12. Consider the possible rewards if the plan is successful.

Step 13. Consider the penalties if the plan fails.

Step 14. Determine the odds in favor of success or failure of the plan.

Step 15. Figure out what the other fellow will do if you carry out the plan.

Step 16. See how many other plans you can find which will take you to the same goal.

Step 17. Use this same procedure (Steps 1 to 15) with each of the other plans. Find the best plan.

Step 18. Go off by yourself and make your decision.

An example of the use of the
decision-making technique

We shall imagine that you are married. You have two boys, 8 and 10. You live in a three-bedroom house. Each boy has his own room.

A close relative asks to come and live with you. He is very old and now lives alone. You must decide whether or not you will allow the relative to move in. This is a reasonably important decision. Here is how you could use the 18 Step Decision-Making Technique:

Step 1. You get all the facts about the situation which suggests the plan.

What capital does the relative have? What income? Is he earning any money? Where and how does he live now? What are the advantages and disadvantages to him, in his present location? Does anyone take care of him now?

Get all the facts about the situation.

Step 2. You get all the facts about the plan.

How will the relative spend his time? Does he require special food? Will he contribute any money towards his support? How dose the relative handle the children? Is he well or ill, good-natured or sullen, even-tempered or crotchety?

Step 3. What is the goal of the plan?

Is the goal to provide basic care for the relative? To keep the relative from being lonesome? To provide help with your housework? To save money?

Step 4. Does the goal of the proposed plan conflict with any of your personal goals?

If your goal is to provide the children with the best possible environment and training, there might be a conflict.

Step 5. Do you have enough general facts in the field of the care and handling of old folks?

If not, get the facts. Get them from books, lectures, and classes or from experts in individual conferences.

Step 6. What is your physical condition and what are your physical qualifications as they bear on the proposed plan?

Are you in a position, physically, to carry out the plan? Are the other members of the family physically able to do their part?

Step 7. Will you have sufficient control of the situation if the relative moves in?

Step 8. Check the proposed plan against your thinking habits.

Are your thoughts restricted to the activities of the children, to the details of your vocation, and to your established family activities? If so, the proposed plan may not fit your thinking habits.

If you habitually think about caring for old people, the plan would fit your thinking habits.

Step 9. Check the proposed plan against your emotional habits. Will your emotions make it easy for you to carry out the plan?

If you are nervous and worried, the plan might not fit your emotional habits. You would have another person to worry about.

If you are calm and relaxed, the plan might fit your emotional habits. To this extent it should be easy for you to execute the plan.

Step 10. Check the plan against your physical habits.

Are you accustomed to taking the family on strenuous weekend trips? Must you take the relative with you? The plan might not fit your physical habits.

On the other hand, if you and your spouse like to go to dances and parties, a built-in baby sitter might be in harmony with your physical habits.

Step 11. Is your environment right for the plan?

You have only three bedrooms. If the relative comes, the boys would have to room together.

You have only one bathroom.

The dining room table is too small for five people.

You have only one TV.

Your environment may not be right for the plan.

Step 12. What are the rewards if the plan is successful?

The relative is well cared for.

Step 13. What are the penalties if the plan fails?

Possibly inconvenience, hard feelings, an upset home, and an unsatisfactory environment for the boys. Possibly a disgruntled relative.

Step 14. What are the chances that the plan will succeed?

The chances should be as large as possible in favor of success. Large odds in favor of failure of the plan would be bad.

Step 15. What will the other fellow do if you carry out the plan?

Are there other relatives who would like to live with you? Would the relative in question stop caring for himself? Would he expect you to accept full responsibility? Would your spouse rebel? Would the children react unfavorably?

Step 16. Can you find any other plans which will reach the same goal?

How about a home for the aged? Could the relative stay where he is if you supplied some money? Could he live with another relative?

Step 17. Use this Decision-Making Technique with each of the other plans you think of.

Try to find a better plan. Even if you like the proposed plan, a better plan would please you more.

Step 18. Now is when you go off by yourself and make your decision.

Give yourself plenty of time. Get away from all influences and pressures. Be sure your physical condition is good. Ignore any desire you may have either to accept or to reject the plan. Be objective. Make your decision on a strictly intellectual basis.

The suggestions

A. Try the Decision-Making Technique on some of your past decisions.

Think back in your life. Select a few decisions you once made which proved to be very *wise*. Go through the 18 Steps of the Decision-Making Technique as though you were back there making the decisions. Had you actually followed the 18 Steps, would you have made the decisions which proved to be so wise?

Next, select some decisions you once made which proved to be very *un*wise. Imagine yourself about to make the decisions. Use the 18 Step Technique. See if, had you used this Decision-Making Technique, you would have made the unwise decisions.

B. List the most important decisions you will need to make in the next month or two. Add others to the list as they occur to you. Keep your list.

Must you always use the complete Decision-Making Technique?

No. Simply consider any suggested plan. Then start with Step 1 of the Decision-Making Technique. Go down the steps until the plan fails to meet the requirements of a certain step. When this occurs, reject the plan.

Many times you can see at a glance that a proposed plan fails to pass one of the first 15 Steps. Reject it!

Caution: Never make a "Yes" decision when you use only part of the full technique. The steps you omit may be the steps which would guide you away from a bad decision.

Chapter 3

HOW TO IMPROVE YOUR ABILITY TO MAKE
WISE DECISIONS

*In this chapter you learn 11 special pro-
cedures. They help you make the best
use of the Decision-Making Technique.*

It may be true that you can't teach an old *dog* new tricks.

But this old saying doesn't apply to humans. A man can learn
new tricks to the last moment of his life.

Would you like to improve your ability to learn a new activity? Here are four things you can do (1) Practice the new
activity. (2) Improve your physical condition. (3) Develop
some habits which will help you perform the new activity. (4)
Learn and use some supplementary techniques.

Improve your ability to make wise decisions

Suppose the new activity you wish to perform is the making
of wise decisions. Then (1) you can improve this ability by
practicing the Decision-Making Technique. (2) If you improve
your physical condition so you think more clearly, you will
improve your ability to make wise decisions. (3) Develop a
new habit, such as always looking for the facts, and this new
habit will help you make wise decisions. (4) Use the right
new technique (the Card System, described below, is a good

31

example), and the new technique will help you make wise decisions.

In this chapter we shall consider some special habits and procedures. You can use them to improve your ability to use the Decision-Making Technique and to make wise decisions.

TO HELP MAKE WISE DECISIONS

1. SET UP THE HABIT OF COLLECTING FACTS

Notice that Steps 1, 2, and 5 of the Decision-Making Technique require you to get important facts.

You know how to gather facts, of course. You have gathered facts all your life. You have established certain fact-gathering habits and procedures.

But possibly your way of gathering the facts, like Topsy, has just "growed." It is good but not perfect.

In any case, try this approach: Think of your ability to gather facts as a distinct skill. Think of it as a special habit you will develop. You will develop the skill and have it ready to help you when you wish to make a wise decision.

Here are some suggestions to improve your ability to get the facts.

First Tip. Be Sure That What You Get Are Really Facts

Many times, when you ask for the facts, people give you their personal opinions, hunches, subjective notions, or guesses.

Often what people give you as fact is tinged and warped by their desires, prejudices, and fears.

Some people like to appear especially intelligent or well-informed. They'll give you a guess or a hunch in such positive language that it sounds like a fact. Other people will give you hearsay, exaggerated statements, and downright lies as facts.

Some people edit the facts. They give you the facts they think you should have. They tell you what you would like to hear.

The story is told about an interesting custom in an oriental country. Let's say a traveler is walking along a road. He asks how far it is to the next town. The inhabitants always give him an answer which is less than the actual number of miles. The theory behind this custom is that the traveler should be happy. If he knows the true distance he might be discouraged.

When someone gives you what appear to be the facts, ask yourself, "Could this person be prejudiced? Does he, or can he, profit in any way from my decision? Is he inclined to exaggerate? Could he make an honest mistake? Does what he says check with my other information? Can I be sure he's giving me the facts?"

Second Tip. Get The Same Facts From Several Sources

An American couple toured the British Isles by bicycle. When they reached a strange town they asked the first four or five likely residents the same question, "Which is the best inn in town?" When two or more residents agreed on one certain inn, that was the one the couple selected. This method gave excellent results.

Another couple, when touring by car, take with them several different books which rate the hotels, motels, and restaurants. When they reach a new city or town they compare the recommendations made by the different books. They choose the hotel, motel, or restaurant which two or more books say is the best.

You can use this procedure in any field where several sources of information are available. For example, do you want the facts about the stock market? Locate several sources of information and compare them.

Third Tip. Check All Written Recommendations

Phone the person who wrote the recommendation and get a verbal report.

Once a man applied for a position. The superintendent said, "Your recommendations are good, but I always check with the writers of the recommendations before I hire anyone." He went on to tell the applicant that he always phoned about a person with a "To whom it may concern" recommendation. When phoned personally, the man who wrote the recommendation might say, "Glad you called me. Don't hire that person, whatever you do."

The recommendation may be written simply to help the person get another position. It may not give any of the important facts about the person.

Fourth Tip. Know The Current Facts In Your Field

Business and professional men must know what is going on in their fields. One example is the lawyer. He must know all the changes in the laws. Another is the doctor. He must know about the new medicines and the latest medical techniques. The businessman must know about the new discoveries in his field, the activities of his competitors, and changes in the economic trend.

Most professional people and businessmen use services of various kinds. The doctors have their professional journals. The businessmen their trade journals. These services supply the current facts.

If such outside helps are available in the fields in which you make important decisions, by all means use them. It takes some of your time to read the reports. It costs a little money. But you'll find it worth the time and the cost if you want to make wise decisions in your vocational field.

When you use these public services you have the same facts as are supplied to all the other workers in the same field. If you want more facts, develop your own private fact-gathering system.

Your private fact-collection system may be local and informal. An attorney, for example, may send a clerk to a certain court to listen and to report the progress of a case. If the attorney is in Washington, he may have his assistant attend a session of the House of Representatives or the Senate. The assistant reports the progress of legislation which is important to the attorney.

J. P. Morgan, the famous banker, used this plan. He sent Bernard Baruch to Brazoria County, Texas. He was to study and bring back the facts concerning a sulphur dome in which Morgan was interested.

Your fact-gathering system may be general, complicated, and highly organized.

When the Rothschilds were growing in power and wealth, they established a large, intricate, and successful system. It gathered the important business and political facts as they developed. These facts were reported to each of the five brothers, in as many different capitals of Europe. The Rothschilds used carriages with false bottoms, letters written in secret code, their own ships, and a great number of trained couriers who traveled constantly over the face of Europe. In the palaces of all the brothers, couriers constantly came and went. A courier might arrive in the night. The Rothschild in residence would be awakened. He would read the message and immediately send off an answer.

Such a system is costly, of course. But it may pay. In the case of the Rothschilds the system brought to Nathan Rothschild, in England, news of the fall of Napoleon hours before the official reports reached London. This enabled Nathan to buy heavily in the stock market and to make millions.

The system you develop to bring you the facts you need may bear no resemblance to that of the Rothschilds. They used their ingenuity and developed a system for their use. Possibly you can use your intelligence and develop a system to meet your needs.

Fifth Tip. Use Graphs For Moving Facts

Many of the facts you gather are stationary. The height of a building and the distance from one place to another are stationary facts. So is a vote of 765 to 43.

But many of the facts you gather will be what we might call "moving" facts. Learn to handle these facts better and you can improve your decision-making ability.

Examples of "moving" facts are the economic condition of the country, the market price of government bonds, a salesman's weekly sales volume, the monthly cost of food for you and your family, the growth rate of the children, and the weekly production of a department in a factory and of the whole factory. Another example is your money in the bank, together with what businessmen call the "cash flow."

When you deal with moving facts, it's a good plan to work with graphs. Put points on the graph paper to show the facts and connect the points with straight lines. The line shows the trend.

To learn more about the use of graphs for moving facts in a business, see any good management consultant. At the same time ask him about "management by exception."

Otherwise see the book, *Modern Elementary Statistics*,[1] by John E. Freund, 2nd edition, Chapter 17.

Keep your graphs up to date. Use your graphs to keep you informed about changes in the important moving facts. Check proposed plans with your graphs before you make your decisions.

Sixth Tip. Don't Be Lazy When The Time Comes To Get The Facts

It's easy to guess, to follow a hunch, to be guided by intuition, or to follow someone's advice.

You may find it a big temptation to jump into action without the facts. You hope for luck, or some person, to pull you out if you make a mistake. Don't do it. You can easily get yourself into a lot of trouble.

Here's an example: A man planned to build an apartment house on a certain lot. He made a half-hearted check of the facts. Everything seemed satisfactory. He bought the lot and applied for a building permit. Then he discovered a ten-foot setback line. He couldn't erect the building he planned. In fact, with the setback line, the lot wasn't suitable for an apartment house at all. He made a big mistake because he didn't get all the important facts.

---

[1] (Englewood Cliffs, N. J.: Prentice-Hall, Inc., 1960).

Don't go on assumptions. Get the facts!

Seventh Tip. Let Someone Help You

Often you can hire someone, or persuade someone, to get the facts for you. This saves your time. Perhaps a friend or a member of your family can help you gather the facts.

Corporations and big investors pay thousands of dollars to people who do nothing but gather and classify facts.

Eighth Tip. Use The Reporter Questions

Who? What? When? Where? Why? and How? are questions used by reporters. They use the list of questions to be sure they get all the important facts.

You can add some of your own—How Many? How Much? How Long? and How Big? for example.

Suppose the proposed plan, for or against which you must decide, is the acceptance of a certain job. You want all the important facts.

The answer to Who? is the name of the company, and possibly the name of the man who will be your superior. What? gives you the duties of the job. When? gives you the starting date. Ask Where? and you have the location. Why? can be why the job is open or why it is offered to you. How? leads you to the way you will have to work and live to carry on the job activities. How Many? can cover the number of other employees, or possibly the number of other people doing the same sort of work. Answer How Much? and you know your starting salary and the increases you may expect. How Long? tells you whether the job is permanent or temporary. Answer How Big? and you know how much you can grow in the proposed job.

Ninth Tip. Test Your Powers Of Recall

Now try this: First get all the facts about the proposed plan and the situation which suggests it. Then sit down with someone who knows the general field. Tell him all about the situation and the plan. Invite questions.

As an example, suppose you have a chance to invest $10,000 in a grocery store. First get all the facts about the situation and the proposed plan. Then sit down with your banker, a professional consultant, or with a successful grocer. Tell him all about the situation and the plan.

Use this procedure. It helps you in two ways. First, when you know you are going to tell someone all about a situation and a plan, you try harder to remember all the facts. Second, when you recite the facts and hear the other person's questions you discover any gaps in your facts.

Tenth Tip. Make A Paragraph Outline

Possibly you need more facts in a certain field. If so, try the following method. It will help you find and remember the important facts in any field.

Find a good book in the field in which you wish to gather your facts.

Read the book a paragraph at a time. When you complete a paragraph, write one sentence which sums up the whole paragraph. Write the sentence on a separate sheet of paper (not in the book). Use a typewriter if you can.

Sometimes one summary sentence can be made to cover several short paragraphs.

Don't read ahead of your writing. Write your summary sentence for each paragraph before you go on to the next paragraph. Do this and you keep your curiosity alive. You wonder what's coming next. This helps keep you going.

When you finish your paragraph outline you have a written condensation of the book. But you have it only on paper. It isn't in *you*. It isn't yet part of your general fund of information.

Now read and re-read your paragraph outline until you know it. Then you will have, in your thinking, all the important facts given in the book. Your general knowledge in the field will be materially increased.

Try this paragraph outline plan. You'll be delighted with the results. Even one paragraph outline of the right book, properly learned, gives you a tremendous number of important facts.

As you use this plan and the one to follow, remember **to**

think of yourself as a collector. You know many people who collect antiques, works of art, old books, or rare coins. Make yourself a champion collector of vital facts in fields in which you make important decisions.

Eleventh Tip. Use The Card System

Here's another excellent method. It helps you remember facts.

Have a print shop cut several hundred little white cards, about 1¾ by 3 inches. Light cardboard scrap can be used. They will cost very little.

Use these cards when you want to remember such facts as numbers, formulae, dates, and foreign words.

On one side of a card write the figures, date, formula, or whatever else you wish to remember. On the other side write a question, to answer which you must give the number, fact, or date on the reverse side. Use a typewriter or write by hand, in ink. For example, if the date you wish to remember is 1492, write that on one side of a card. Write the question "Columbus discovered America?" on the other side. Or write, "straight line" on one side. Write, "? is shortest distance between two points?" on the other side of the card. Or write "la mesa" on one side and "table" on the other, if you want to learn Spanish vocabulary.

Put all your cards pertaining to one subjet together. Or mix the cards if you wish. Arrange them with the questions up. This is your "Daily Pile."

Now read the question on the top card and, without looking at the reverse side, answer the question. If you can't give the answer, study the answer on the back of the card and put the card on the bottom of the pile. If you can give the answer without looking at the back of the card, put the card in a box marked "Sunday." Or mark the box for any day of the week when you can take the time to review the cards.

Go through your Daily Pile in this way until you can give the answer to each question without looking at the back of the card. Then all your cards will be in the "Sunday Box."

As fast as you make new cards, put them in your Daily Pile. As fast as you can remember the answers to the questions, put the cards in the Sunday Box.

You can carry the cards with you, fastened together with a rubber band. You can then quiz yourself at odd moments. Put the cards you learn in a pocket or purse ready for your Sunday Box when you get home.

When Sunday comes, go through all the cards in your Sunday Box. Those you don't know, put back into your Daily Pile. Those you know without looking at the backs of the cards put in a box marked "Monthly Box."

At the end of each month, go through your Monthly Box. Those you know put in a box marked "Six Month Box." Those you don't know, return to the Daily Pile.

When a card graduates from the Six Month Box, you know the fact. You may keep the card for later review or throw it away.

What happens when you use this plan?

First, you enjoy adding new cards to your Daily Pile. Try to add several every day. You can write your cards when you don't feel like memorizing.

Second, you enjoy quizzing yourself.

Third, use the system and you can be sure you will learn each fact you put into your Daily Pile. This is because a good way to remember something is to learn it, forget it, learn it again, forget it again, and finally learn it again.

Do you happen to be one of the millions of bridge fans? If so, and if you would like to play better bridge, try the card system. When you make a mistake while playing, make a quick note of it. When you get home put the correct procedure and the appropriate question on a card. Do this for all your mistakes. Then study your cards.

You can see what this will do for you. Most bridge players make the same mistakes over and over. You can get yourself out of this class very quickly.

Now you have two methods for remembering facts in any field. The card method is best when you want to learn short, specific facts such as dates, formulas, new words, foreign vocabulary, and rules. The paragraph outline method is best when you want to remember the gist of a book. You can use both methods together.

Twelfth Tip. Get A Good General Education

When you have a good general education you have many facts in many different fields.

You get your general education partly in school. You can get even a larger part of it after you leave school.

Read in a variety of fields. Use the paragraph outline plan and the card system to help you remember what you read.

Make a paragraph outline of a recommended book in business law, for instance, and learn your outline. Use the card system where indicated.

Do the same for good books in the fields of health, psychology, business administration, economics, writing, public speaking, human relations (getting along with people), politics, marriage relations, child rearing, and travel, to name a few. Follow this plan. Forever after you will find it easier to understand problems, to find solutions to problems, and to make wise decisions in the fields in which you have gathered the facts.

2. ESTABLISH YOUR PERSONAL GOALS

To be ready for Step 4 of our Decision-Making Technique, you must establish your personal goals.

The Fields Of Action

Most of your goals will be in these fields: Health, human relations, the emotional field, marriage, family and child rearing, vocational, financial, recreation and sports, the religious field, the field of morals and ethics.

The Possible Goals

Here are some possible goals: To have and keep excellent health. To get along well with people and to deal with them effectively. To show emotional stability at all times. To have a very successful marriage. To have a happy and well-disciplined family. To be in the top 10 percent in your vocation. To accumulate $100,000. To excel in some sport or game. To be an outstanding religious worker. To behave, at all times, in a most ethical and moral manner.

Also, for any certain field you can elect to have no goal. You can simply ignore the field and the activities in it.

How To Select Your Goals

List the fields given above under "Fields of Action," in a column. To the right of each field write your goal for that field. If you don't have a goal for the field, just skip it. For example:

Field	*Goals*
Health	Get and keep excellent health
Human Relations	Get along well with people
Emotional	
Marriage	Very successful marriage
Family and Child Rearing	Happy, healthy and well-trained children
Vocational	Become a doctor
Financial	
Recreation and Sports	
Religion	
Morals and Ethics	

This person has five goals. Any suggested plan would get a black mark in Step 4 of the Decision-Making Technique if it promised to interfere with his efforts (1) to achieve an excellent physical condition, (2) to develop harmonious and successful human relations, (3) to maintain his excellent marriage adjustment, (4) to promote his happy home and his well-trained children, and (5) if it would interfere with his vocational activities.

Here is another example:

Field	Goals
Health	Excellent health
Human Relations	
Emotional	
Marriage	
Family and Child Rearing	
Vocational	Become an executive
Financial	
Recreational and Sports	Play golf in the 70's
Religion	
Morals and Ethics	

Here the person has three goals. He would look with great suspicion on any plan which might interfere with his health, his vocational success, or his ability to play outstanding golf.

Determine Your Goals

List the fields of action. Then write in *your* goals.

To do this you must take some time from other things you like to do. You must do some important thinking. You may have to talk about some of your goals with other people and come to an understanding. All this requires a little time and effort. But right now, take the time and make the effort. You'll find it both rewarding and interesting.

Check Your Goals

Now look at each of your goals. Answer these questions: Would you really enjoy the situation or condition you have set up as your goal? Are you willing to spend the time, effort, and money necessary to reach your goal?

Remember, you need to know your goals to advance yourself and to get more out of life. You need them to help you make wise decisions (Step 4).

Keep your list of goals. You will need it every time you use the Decision-Making Technique.

3. WATCH FOR HIDDEN OBJECTIVES

A hidden objective often appears in connection with a plan.

The plan has a stated goal. This goal is announced. It is easy to see it.

At the same time the person who proposes the plan may have his own unstated objective. This hidden objective is usually something of special benefit to the person who proposes the plan.

Locate The Hidden Objectives Of Other People

Many people have hidden objectives when they suggest a plan.

Let's say that you are traveling in a foreign country. You meet a very charming man. He is handsome, polite, and considerate. He is excellent company.

It gradually becomes known that he has a plan by which you can invest $12,000 (which you have available) in a business. If the business has this extra capital, it can get a special license and buy out a rival concern. Then the company will have a monopoly in the manufacture of much-needed items.

You are promised a profit of $3,000 a year, with perfect safety, and all your money back in three years.

What might be the hidden objective of the man who proposes the plan? Could it be to get your money away from you and into his hands for his own use?

What should you do when you locate (or suspect) another person's private objective? If the hidden objective, when reached, will bring loss or inconvenience to you, you may wish to reject the plan.

Should You Have An Attitude Of Suspicion?

Do you think the above implies a cynical attitude toward the motives of other people? If so, remember that it's better to be cynical than gullible! William Allen White, the famous editor, used to say, "It pays to be a little suspicious of everybody."

Remember, too, that people respect you when you make wise decisions. This is true even when you outwit them in their attempts to deceive you. But when you make a bad decision, even if other people benefit at your expense, they lose respect for you.

Always look for possible hidden objectives.

Locate Your Own Hidden Objectives

You must also consider your own hidden goals.

Suppose you suddenly invest your savings in one of the mutual funds. You say you did it to have your money handled by professionals. This is the published goal of the plan. Your hidden objective may be to stop the activities of someone who is urging you to lend him the money.

Or, let us say, you join the local country club. You tell everyone you joined in order to play golf. But your hidden objective may be more social contacts. Possibly, if you are a salesman, your hidden objective may be to find some excellent prospects.

What should you do when you locate one of your hidden objectives? First examine it. Is it detrimental to anyone else? If so, eliminate it. Otherwise see if you should make the hidden objective a real goal and try to achieve it openly. If you should, go to Steps 16 and 17 of the Decision-Making Technique. See if you can find a better way to reach your goal. In the Country Club example you might find a better and less expensive way to locate social contacts, or a better way to find prospects.

Study your own private objectives. The practice will help you uncover the private objectives of other people.

4. DON'T LET OTHER PEOPLE FOOL YOU

You should find it easy to determine the rewards of the proposed plan (Step 12). The person who proposes the plan usually emphasizes the rewards.

But remember that many people exaggerate. In his enthusiasm, the person who proposes the plan may make the possible rewards appear much greater than they really are.

Be on the lookout for this type of exaggeration. Be a little
skeptical. Usually it pays to cut the promised rewards by a
fourth, or even by half or more, just to be on the safe side.

One man bought a grocery business. The seller assured him
that he would make a net profit of $10,000 the first year. To be
conservative, however, the buyer estimated no profit, but a
break-even for the first year. He made sure he could carry
his family for that period. He was wise. Unexpected complica-
tions arose. The net profit for the first year was only $1,000!

5. DON'T FOOL YOURSELF

In many cases *you* think of the plan. Can you count on yourself to see the possible rewards as they really are? Not necessarily.

Underestimate The Rewards

Are you inclined to be optimistic? Then you may tend to
exaggerate the possible rewards. If so, estimate the possible
rewards of your wonderful plan as a half or a fourth of what
you hope they will be.

Overestimate The Penalties

The penalties (Step 13), should the plan fail, are usually
not so well advertised as are the rewards. But you can still
determine the possible penalties without too much trouble.

First see the penalties for failure as you think they will be.
Then estimate them to be greater.

Mr. Jones, let us say, thinks about buying a franchise to sell
a certain product in a selected territory. When he comes to
Step 13, he considers his possible loss in case of failure. Mr.
Jones is sure the plan will succeed. He is sure he will enjoy the
work, render a needed service, and make a lot of money. He
can't see how he can possibly fail. Nevertheless he faces up to
the possibility of a loss. He thinks the worst that can happen
is that he might just break even. Then he looks again. Now he

sees that, should his plan fail, he might actually lose his entire investment.

When you figure the possible penalties, should the proposed plan fail, try to be objective. Try to see the penalties exactly as they may be. Then, especially if you tend to be optimistic, exaggerate the possible loss.

6. LEARN TO FIGURE THE ODDS

Many of your decisions will hinge on the odds (Step 14).

One way to improve your decision-making ability is to become adept at figuring the odds.

The easy way to figure the odds is by the use of mathematics.

Suppose you try to find a certain house. You don't know the house number but you know the block. There are 13 houses in the block. You can, then, go to any house and have 1 chance in 13 of reaching the house you want.

Many times, however, you don't have the figures. Then you can't figure the odds mathematically. You must guess. In such a case you can figure the odds as "small," "even," or "great." Small could be 4 or 5 chances in 100. Medium could be about 50–50. Great could be 80 or 90 chances out of 100.

You can practice in connection with many of the decisions you make throughout the day.

Do you contemplate dallying another three minutes over your breakfast coffee? If you do, what are the odds that you will *miss* your train to the city? Are the odds *great*?

Did you slice your drive into the rough? If you use a short iron from the rough, are the odds *great* that you will get your ball onto the fairway? If you use a three wood from the rough, are the odds *small* that you'll pull off a long shot and put your ball on the green?

If you go to the boss without preparation and ask for a raise, what are the odds in favor of success? Are they small? Even? But suppose you work up a little presentation and you give it to the boss. Then what do you think the odds will be that you get the raise?

Are you about to double your opponents when playing bridge? Figure the odds in favor of a set.

You want to spend your vacation fishing. What are the odds that you can persuade the family to agree to the plan? Small? Even? Great?

Practice in this way. You can become proficient at figuring the odds.

Allow For Your Desires

Here's another way you can improve your ability to determine the odds. Make allowances for your wants and desires!

Are you eager to adopt a certain plan? For example, are you in love? Do you want to marry someone? Then it's easy to be swayed by your desires. You tend to figure the odds too high for a successful marriage and too low for failure.

Here is a good rule: When you want very much to carry out some plan, *underestimate* the odds for success and *overestimate* the odds for failure.

When you get a little money ahead (or a lot of money) there is always someone ready to show you how to "invest" it. The person who proposes the plan makes it sound very attractive. He may bring much pressure to bear on you. This is an especially good time to figure the odds for success as *less* than they appear.

If you have a strong desire to follow a proposed plan, always minimize the odds in favor of success. In this way you can balance off your enthusiasm for the plan. You can improve your batting average for wise decisions.

7. Learn To Anticipate The Reactions Of Other People

To improve your ability to use Step 15 of the Decision-Making Technique, increase your knowledge and understanding of people.

Associate with people. Keep your eyes and ears open. Learn

about people. All this will help you guess how the other fellow will react.

It is possible, however, to deal with people all your life and never really learn much about them. This is because, in general, you see what you are trained to see. So get the right training. Learn to understand the psychological reactions, kinks, quirks, and needs of the average person. Do this and you will be pleased with the improvement in your ability to guess how the other fellow will react to any proposed plan.

8. Don't Let Them Rush You Into An Unwise Decision

Another easy way to improve your decision-making ability is this: Don't let anyone rush you into a decision! Take plenty of time for the whole Decision-Making Technique and Step 18.

There are two situations in which people try to rush you. One is when you show some interest in something for sale.

You ask the price of a lot, for instance. Immediately you learn that you have arrived just in time. The price is about to be raised! Or the owner is about to take the property off the market. Decide now! This is your last chance!

Did you ever notice how often, when you ask about something for sale, you happened to arrive "just in the nick of time"? Only a few choice houses in the tract remain to be sold! This is almost the last ticket for the performance! Just a few units remain at this price! The price of the stock will advance next week when the company makes a special announcement! If you want this bargain you must decide immediately!

Don't let yourself be rushed into a snap decision!

Sometimes, of course, you have known about the offering for some time. You procrastinated. Finally you got around to it. It can easily be that you did arrive just in time to get in under the wire. In such a case remember it was your fault for not starting sooner. Don't compound the error by making a snap decision just because you arrived late.

In any case, if anyone tries to rush you, just remember this:

It may be better to miss a genuine opportunity once in a while than to make a bad decision.

Here is the second situation in which people may try to rush you. It's when someone comes to you with a special opportunity.

Does somebody want you to decide at once? Does he want you to take advantage of a wonderful offer which will soon be withdrawn? If so, think a little. First, realize that you want to make a wise decision and not a snap decision. Second, ask yourself this: Whose fault is it if the person comes to you so late? Whose fault is it if he doesn't allow you time to use the full Decision-Making Technique? Is it your fault? No. It's the other person's fault. So don't feel that you must make a snap decision. If the other person wants you to make a decision, let him give you time to use the Decision-Making Technique.

There are situations, of course, when someone happens onto an exceptional opportunity unexpectedly. If he offers it to you, you may have to act quickly if you want it. In such a case, either be prepared to make a quick and wise decision or let it pass. It's better to miss an opportunity once in a while than to make an unwise decision.

Whenever you are rushed in any way and you are tempted to make a snap decision, refuse to do so. Always use the 18 Step Decision-Making Technique and make wise decisions.

Ask, "Whose Decision Is This?"

In Step 18 ask, "Whose decision is this?"

Answer, "This is my decision. Since it's my decision *I'm* going to make it, not someone else. So I'll just forget, for the time being, all the people who are eager to have me decide in favor of this plan, or against it. I'll put them out of my thinking entirely. I'll consider this matter strictly on its merits. I'll go by the facts."

9. DON'T RUSH YOURSELF INTO AN UNWISE DECISION

When a situation calls for action, you may be tempted to rush in with a half-baked plan. Don't do it. It will pay you to take some extra time, use the 18 Steps, and find a really good plan.

Mrs. Jones drove 100 miles in her car to visit her mother. Mr. Jones drove his own car and joined his wife at the end of the week. Over the week end Mr. Jones used his wife's car. When he left for home Sunday night he drove off in his car, with the keys to his wife's car in his pocket. When he got home he discovered his wife's car keys. He didn't want her to be without the use of her car. He blamed himself for his stupidity. So he immediately got into his car and drove the 200-mile round trip to return the keys.

Now suppose that, when Mr. Jones got home and discovered his wife's keys in his pocket, he had sat down quietly and used the 18 step technique. Don't you think that, when he reached Step 16, he would have found a better plan? He would have realized that he could telephone his wife and instruct her to get the keys for her car from the local dealer. Or a locksmith could make her a key.

In this way he could have saved money, time, and effort.

10. If You Are Prone To Say "Yes"

Many people say "Yes" almost by habit. It's much easier for them to say "Yes" to a proposed plan than it is to decide against it. The result is that they accept many plans they should reject. They make many bad decisions.

If you happen to be one of these people, practice saying "No." Get used to turning down plans suggested by other people. This may bother you at first. But you soon get used to it. If a person suggests that you go to a movie, for example, say "No" just for the practice. Then suggest something else to do.

11. Be Objective

When you are objective, you see things, think about them, talk about them, and react to them as they actually are.

If you say the car is going 25 miles an hour (you see it on the speedometer), you make an objective statement. When you say there are 17 people at the meeting (you counted them), you are being objective.

On the other hand, you are being subjective if you make a statement which expresses a judgment. For example, you say, "The car is going fast." Or you say, "There was a fair-sized crowd at the meeting."

Let us say that someone asks you for a description of Mr. X. You say, "He is six feet tall, has light brown hair, a dark skin, and brown eyes. The last time I saw him he wore a brown suit." Then you make an objective statement.

You make subjective statements if you react as did the man on the witness stand when questioned by a lawyer.

Lawyer: "Please describe Mr. X."

Witness: "He's a gyp artist."

Lawyer: "Please. I'm not asking you for your personal opinion of Mr. X. I'm asking for a *description* of him."

Witness: "That's what I just gave you. He's a gyp artist."

Lawyer: "But don't you see, you didn't give me a description of Mr. X. You just told me what you thought of him."

Witness: "Certainly I gave you a description of Mr. X. My opinion hasn't anything to do with it. He's just naturally a gyp artist. That's all there is to it!"

You are objective when you react to facts calmly and when you deal with the facts as they are.

Suppose a doctor tells you that you have some physical trouble. You take the news calmly and start the proper line of treatment. Then you are being objective.

You are being subjective if a doctor tells you that there is something wrong with you, and you get frightened and excited.

When you make a decision, (1) try to get the actual facts. Insist on objective statements. (2) Act on the facts in an objective, and not in a subjective, manner. Don't fly off the handle. Make your decisions and carry them out in a calm, workmanlike manner.

Catch Them While They're Small

Here's something you can do to help you be more objective.

Use the 18 Step Decision-Making Technique before your desires develop. Then it's easier to be objective.

A young lady, for example, meets a certain man. She is strongly attracted to him. He, in turn, seems to like her very much. Immediately she considers the possibility of a marriage proposal. She uses the Decision-Making Technique. She sees that her decision should be "No." She makes her decision *before* the proposal, and before she gets too interested. Then she develops a good strong set *against* marriage with the man.

If she delays her decision until after she falls in love with the man, and until after he proposes, her desires may prevent a wise decision. She may not be able to say "No" at all. She may find herself in a bushel of marital trouble.

Think of all the trouble from which you can save yourself if you use the Decision-Making Technique before strong emotions develop within you!

Never Rationalize

When you decide on a course of action be objective. Act on the facts. You may, however, *want* to do something which is not in strict harmony with the facts. Then it's a temptation to ignore the facts.

You may want a new automobile, for example, to replace your old one. Let's say that you can't afford the monthly payments on the new car.

You don't want to come right out and say, "If I undertake the monthly payments I may run short of money and get myself into trouble. The car might even be repossessed. But I want the new car, so I'll buy it anyway, although I know it's a foolish thing to do."

Instead of that you may say, "I can cut down on some of my luxuries and save some money. That will be easy when I have a new car. Also, if I have a new car I'll save on repairs, gas, and oil. What I save will go a long way toward making

the payments. So if I buy the new car it really is a wise investment."

That is rationalizing. When you rationalize you find good
excuses for doing what you *want* to do, but which you know
you really *shouldn't* do.

Never rationalize. No matter what your wants and desires
may be, always act on the exact facts. Always be objective.

Be Objective For A Day

Occasionally practice this exercise: Be objective for a whole
day.

On this day, when you act, act on the facts.

See if, for a whole day, you can base all your actions entirely
on the facts and not on your feelings or desires.

For a day, be absolutely and everlastingly objective.

Be Especially Objective In Step 18

The above exercise will help you in Step 18. In this Step it
is very important to be objective. You must not see the facts as
you hope they are, as you would like to have them, or as you
wish they were. You must see the plan, the situation, and all
the facts exactly as they are.

Try this, too, in Step 18: Say to yourself, "Whether or not *I*
want to follow this plan doesn't make any difference. My desires change. What I really want is a wise decision and the
right plan. If I don't care for the plan now, I can learn to like
it. This will be easy if it's a good plan. So I must be sure to
choose the right plan. Then I'll have a wise decision, a good
plan, and I will also *like* the plan."

Ask "Who Suggested The Plan?"

When, in Step 18, you start to make your final decision for
or against a proposed plan, ask yourself, "Did this plan come
logically from my own activities? Or did someone else propose
this plan? Does this plan come more or less 'out of the blue'?"

Did someone else propose the plan? Then realize that you
are under no obligation to decide for the plan just because it is
proposed by someone you like or admire.

Always make your own decisions! Make them according to the facts. Be objective!

SUMMARY

The following procedures, techniques, and exercises have been suggested: (1) Establish the habit of collecting facts. (2) Establish your personal goals. (3) Watch for hidden objectives. (4) Don't let other people fool you. (5) Don't fool yourself. (6) Learn to figure the odds. (7) Learn to anticipate the reactions of other people. (8) Don't let them rush you into an unwise decision. (9) Don't rush yourself into unwise decisions. (10) What to do if you are prone to say "Yes." (11) Be objective.

These eleven suggestions should help you use the Decision-Making Technique correctly. Follow the suggestions. Practice the exercises.

In addition, for Step 6 see Chapters 6 and 7.

For special help with Steps 8, 9, and 10 see Chapters 4 and 5.

For Step 15 you will be interested in Chapter 4.

The suggestions

You should be ready, now, to try the Decision-Making Technique with a few of your important decisions. But you can't give the technique a real trial if you must read the list of Steps every time you use them. To give the technique a proper trial you must *know* the Steps.

A. Refer to the list of Steps which starts on page 25. Memorize the Steps and the number of each Step. Memorize them so you can give the number which goes with each Step and name the Step which goes with each number.

Use whatever memory system you like best.

If you don't have a system, turn back to page 39. Use the Card System.

Put the number on one side of a card. Write the Step on the back. Do this for each Step. Then study the cards as directed.

Soon, like a flash, you can give the number of each Step and the Step which goes with each number. Then you can use the Steps in the excitement of a really important decision.

Memorize the Steps right now. Don't read beyond this point until you have memorized them all.

B. As soon as you have memorized the 18 Steps, use the Decision-Making Technique with all your current decisions.

See if you like the technique. See if it works. See if you can depend on it. If so, you have a method you can use all the rest of your life. You have a procedure which will help you get the most out of life and, at the same time, keep you out of much trouble.

C. While you use the Decision-Making Technique with your current decisions, read the next two chapters. In those chapters you will get the facts in an important field. You will also learn another proposed plan. The facts and the plan will help you get the most out of life. They will help you keep yourself out of trouble. They will also help you make wise decisions. Especially is this true when you make decisions concerning people.

D. What should you do if, after a few days, you have *not* memorized the 18 Steps of the Decision-Making Technique? Turn to Chapter 4 and read it carefully. When you come to the end of the chapter, follow the *Instructions if you have not yet learned the 18 steps.*

Chapter 4

THE TRUTH AND NOTHING BUT THE TRUTH
ABOUT YOUR BEHAVIOR

*In this chapter you learn how to make
yourself do what you know you should
do. You also learn how to keep yourself
from doing what you know you should
not do.*

The right habits give you power.

The more good habits you have, the more power you have.
The more power you have, the more you can get from life.

It is now proposed that you establish all the new habits you
need to get the most out of life.

It is also proposed that you stop all your present habits which
get you into trouble. These habits, and the resulting troubles,
do two things. They bring you what you *don't* want from life.
They make it harder to get what you *do* want.

How do you react to these proposals?

You may think it impossible to control your habits. But you
will not make a snap decision. Instead you will get the facts.
You will learn all about the proposed plan. You will use the
Decision-Making Technique. You will make a wise decision.

When you look for the facts about habits, you make an inter-

esting discovery. You find that, to understand your habits, you
must forget all about them! You must first get all the facts about
your *behavior*. The reason is clear. Your habits are simply one
form of your behavior, which is basic.

The facts you need are spread among many books and lectures. The books were printed and the lectures given during
the past 35 or 40 years. It isn't easy to get all the important
facts.

Learn the facts given in this chapter. Then add the facts
you gather from your own study. In the end you will have a
large body of exact facts in this important field of human behavior.

What are some of the important facts?

To start with:

All your information about the world around you comes from your outer covering

That seems wrong, doesn't it? It seems to you that you see a
tree, for instance. But actually, in a sense, you don't see the
tree at all!

Imagine yourself standing near a small tree. Light is reflected
from the tree to your eyes. You "see" the tree.

But suppose you put a screen between yourself and the tree.
Then what? Now the light is reflected from the tree, but it's
stopped by the screen. The light doesn't reach your eyes. You
don't see the tree.

Take away the screen and put your hands before your eyes.
Now the light, reflected from the tree, comes nearer to your
eyes. But still it doesn't reach them. It's stopped by your hands.
You still don't see the tree.

Not until the reflected light actually reaches your eyes can
you see the tree! How do you "see" it? You react to the changes
in your eyes.

In a similar way, you react to changes in your other sense

organs and not to things outside. This may seem to you like an unnecessary distinction. Actually you will soon see how important it is.

Suppose you lie down in a quiet room which is completely dark. Soon you feel a pressure on your chest. What is it? It all depends. You wait for more information from your senses while you try to figure out what's going on.

You feel another pressure on your chest. Still you have no clue. Then you feel a light brush against your cheek. What can it be? Finally from your ears comes what you recognize as a purr. That's it. The cat! Walking on your chest!

You realize that what you know about the outside world comes only from your outer covering. You never contact anything beyond it.

You are like a submarine gliding under the surface of the ocean. The submarine's radar screens, radio receiving sets, sonic depth finder, and other equipment tell the crew of the submarine what is going on outside. In the same way, you move around in your surroundings, and your sense organs on your exterior surface report what is going on outside.

How you operate—your receptors, effectors, stimuli, and the signals

Sense organs such as your eyes, ears, nose, lips, skin, and tongue are scattered around your surface. These are known as "receptors." This is easy to remember because your eyes, ears, skin, nose, and tongue are "receivers" of information from the outside world.

Each receptor is connected by a nerve to your brain. Other nerves go out from your brain to your muscles, organs, and glands. Figure 1. These are called "effectors." You can remember this because your muscles produce an "effect" in your environment.

All around you is your environment. Your environment is

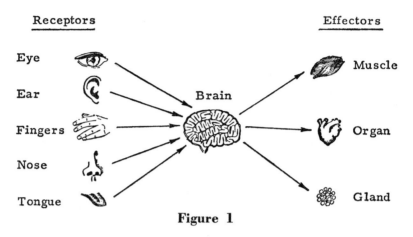

Figure 1

full of objects and people. They do things to you. They affect you in some way. The man next to you spills something on you, for example. Or he gives you a pleasant smile.

We need a name for these things in your environment which affect you. Why not use the word "signal"? The liquid spilled on you is a "signal." The pleasant smile is a "signal."

A signal brings about a change in one or more of your receptors. The change in your receptors is the "stimulus." This term is also easy to remember because the change in your receptor "stimulates," or starts, the nerve impulse toward your brain.

A signal is anything outside you that affects one of your receptors so as to bring about a change in it (the stimulus). Then nerve impulses are sent from your receptor through your brain to your effectors. See Figure 2.

The stimulus (change in a receptor) sends nerve impulses to and through your brain and out again to one of your effectors, in which it brings about a change. The change in your effector might be a muscle movement or one of your glands might secrete a hormone. This change in your effector is the "response."

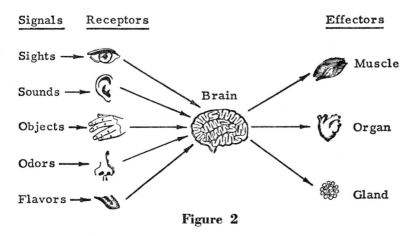

Figure 2

Your stimulus-response mechanism is very important

This stimulus-response action is the foundation of all your behavior. Everything you do is a matter of stimulus and response.

Suppose you hear a yell. You turn to see who is calling. This is what happens: The yell (the signal) brings about a change (the stimulus) in your ear. The change (the stimulus) sends a nerve impulse to your brain and on through your brain to your muscles. Your muscles then turn you towards the sound. This turning is the response.

If you bite into something good and ask for more, this is what goes on: The food (the signal) brings about a change (the stimulus) in your mouth. The change (stimulus) sends nerve impulses to and through your brain and out to your jaw, lips, lungs, and vocal muscles. These operate to say the words, "Please give me another piece." This is your response.

This action from the stimulus to the response is strictly automatic. You, all of you inside your outer covering, have nothing to do with it except to provide the receptors, the nerves, your brain, and the effectors.

You are like a telephone exchange

Your brain and nervous system work together much like a telephone system.

Have you ever seen the central machinery of the automatic dial telephone? You see a machine which sends up a metal rod to various switches as the subscriber dials a number. The rod and switches move according to the number dialed. When the rod stops, the connection is made with the proper telephone in the outgoing system. Then the bell rings in the telephone being called.

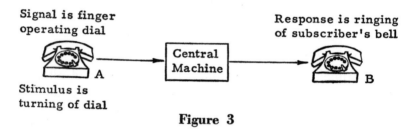

Signal is finger
operating dial

Response is ringing
of subscriber's bell

Central
Machine

A

B

Stimulus is
turning of dial

Figure 3

In Figure 3, telephone A is the receptor. The central machine represents the brain. The telephone called B, where the bell sounds, represents the effector.

Now imagine a dial telephone system so set up that everything is in perfect condition in the central machinery. But the wires leading *to* the central machine are cut. Now dial a number on phones A, B, or C in Figure 4. No telephone bell rings at D, E, or F because no electrical impulses reach the central machine.

Imagine a man with his usual supply of eyes, ears, skin, nose, and mouth. But suppose the nerves between his receptors and his brain are seriously damaged or diseased. Now no message reaches the man's brain and he can't respond to the stimuli. He just lies still. See Figure 5.

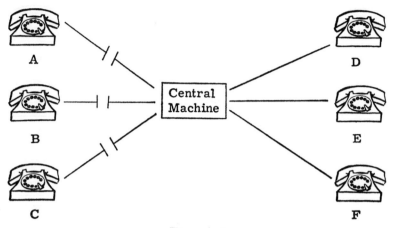

Figure 4

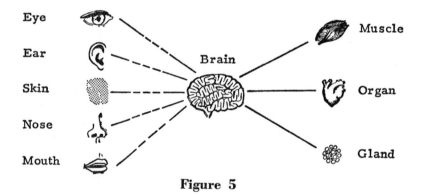

Figure 5

Next, think of a telephone system with wires leading to the central machine. But all the wires going from the central machine to the other phones have been cut. Figure 6.

Dial a number at telephone A, and the rod goes up in the central machine as usual. But that is all. There is no ring at telephone D, E, or F.

Imagine a man with eyes, ears, and fingers. Stimuli in these receptors send nerve messages to the brain in the usual manner.

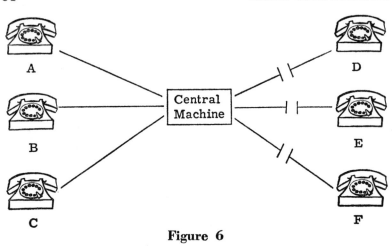

Figure 6

But suppose the man's nerves, running from his brain to his effectors, are diseased or damaged. The damage might come from an injury or from the deterioration of the nerve cells. Then the nerve impulses can't go from the brain to the effectors (Figure 7). No matter what the man sees, hears, or feels, no muscle, organ, or gland is roused to action. The man is as though paralyzed. Since no muscle can be made to act, the man can not eat, walk, or talk. He is like the telephone system in Figure 6.

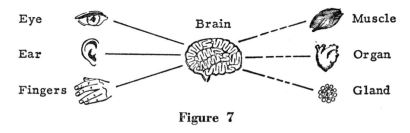

Figure 7

Now suppose you damage the central machine in Figure 3. Then calls cannot go through it from telephone A to telephone B. And in Figure 2, if you damage the brain, the nerve impulses from the receptors to the effectors will be slowed down or stopped. This is true no matter how good the nerves or the receptors and effectors may be.

Also, think what happens if telephone A, in Figure 3, is damaged and out of commission. Then it will send no electrical impulses to the Central Machine. The bell will not ring in telephone B.

Or suppose everything is all right in telephone A and the Central Machine, but telephone B is broken. Then the message can go from telephone A to telephone B but B can't respond.

You can see that it works in exactly the same way inside you. If your hand is hurt or numb so it can't pick up the signals (you can't feel anything) it can't send any message to your brain. Then you can't react to the signal. Also, suppose your leg muscles are so tired or cold that you can't move them. Then your eyes could send messages to your brain, reporting danger, but you couldn't run because your effectors (your legs) wouldn't move.

If you want a telephone bell to ring, you must get the electricity from the subscriber's phone to the central machine and out again to another phone, which must be in good condition.

If you want one of your effectors to operate, you must make the impulses go from a receptor to the brain and out again to the effector, which must be in good condition.

The stimulus-response arc is basic

The circuit from the receptor through the brain and to the effector (from the stimulus to the response) is known as the stimulus-response *arc*. Remember this. It's the backbone of human behavior!

Here's an easy way to see the stimulus-response arc in action. Simply touch a hot stove! The hot stove (signal) brings about changes in your skin (stimulus). As a result of the stimulus, the electrical wave goes over your nerves from your finger to your brain and immediately out again to the proper muscles.

The muscles contract and pull your finger from the hot stove. This is the response. The whole circuit, from your receptor through your brain to the effector, is the stimulus-response arc. If you don't think it's automatic, touch your finger to a piece of hot metal and see what happens!

How to control your actions

Your stimulus-response arcs account for all of your behavior. Now you know exactly what you must do to get yourself to do something. You also know what you must do to keep yourself *from* performing some act. You must control your stimulus-response arcs!

The procedures you need to follow to control your stimulus-response arcs are divided into two groups. One group tells you what to do when you want to *establish* a stimulus-response arc—when you want to make yourself *do* something. The other group tells you what to do when you want to *stop* a stimulus-response arc—when you want to keep yourself *from* doing something.

TEN KEYS TO ESTABLISH STIMULUS-RESPONSE ARCS
(Ten Ways To Make Yourself Do Something)

Key No. 1. You Can Start Stimulus-Response Arcs You Want With Signals

From the first part of this chapter you know that many acts are started by signals. You also know this from personal experience.

Now see if you can put your knowledge to practical use. See if you can start any arc you want simply by setting up a signal.

First decide on the arc you want. Select any act you wish. Suppose you choose the act of reading this book for half an hour before you go to bed tomorrow night.

Now set up a signal to start the arc you want. Make a sign which says, "Read the book for half an hour just before you go to bed." Or it may say, "Remember to read the book." Put the sign where you will see it often.

Try this suggestion. See to what extent the one signal influences you to read the book tomorrow evening before you go to bed.

Yes, this experiment is a little bother. But do it anyway. It's worth the effort. Try it just as a psychological experiment. Learn the technique! Remember, if you want to keep yourself out of trouble and get what you want out of life, you must be able to control yourself and your actions. This is the first step. Be sure to take it.

Now put this book down. Read no more until you have put up your signal.

Is this all you must do to get yourself to perform some act? Is it only necessary to set up a signal and react to it often? Will this make you do whatever you wish? Not necessarily. And not always. There will be times when you will need only one signal to get yourself to carry out the desired act. You simply set up the right signal and you respond by performing the act.

Actually, however, the signal simply *inclines* you to act in a certain direction. If there is little or no resistance, you will carry out the act. If many contrary factors operate so that your proposed arc encounters much resistance, one signal may not bring the act you want. You may have to use several signals. Sometimes even a group of signals is not sufficient. You may have to use all ten of the Keys!

When you use these ten Keys it's much like moving a stalled automobile. One person pushes. If the car is on a slight downgrade so there isn't much resistance, the one person may be enough. He pushes the car easily. But if the car is on a level or on a slight upgrade, the one person may need some help. Then you can add another person. The car moves still more. Put enough people behind the car, each pushing his share, and the car moves as you wish.

Here is the rule: Use as many signals and as many of the ten Keys as you need to get the act you want.

Key No. 2. You Can Make The Arcs Stronger By Adding Signals

You pay more attention to a loud shout than to a whisper. You are more likely to react to a big, bright, or loud signal than to one which is small and hard to see or hear.

Also, two or more signals which operate in the same direction at the same time are more likely to bring about a certain stimulus-response arc. You are then more inclined to carry out the act. Experiment a little. See how you react to one, two, three, four, and then five signals, all pushing you in the same direction. See how you react to weak signals. Then try some strong signals. Try several weak signals together. See if you are more inclined to obey the signals if you use several strong and commanding signals at the same time.

Here are some suggestions:

Put this book where you will see it often. The book itself can act as a signal.

If you have a tape recorder, you can make a tape which says, over and over, "Be sure to read *How To Work Miracles In Your Life* for half an hour before you go to bed." Have your recorder play this message over and over while you prepare for bed tonight and while you dress in the morning.

Perhaps you can persuade someone to remind you. The person may say, occasionally, "Remember your plan to read in the book before you go to bed." The signal another person can give you can be very important.

Years ago Oimet, the famous golfer, used this procedure in an important match. He had his caddy stand by him for every shot. As Oimet prepared to swing, the caddy recited, "Take your time. You have all day. Keep your eye on the ball." Oimet won.

Experiment. Soon you will learn the kind, size, loudness,

brightness, number, and combination of signals you should use for the best results.

As you experiment you may find that you are less inclined to read this book before you go to sleep at night (1) if you use only one signal; (2) if your signals are small, drab, and poorly lighted; (3) if this book is out of sight; (4) if your tape recorder is not ready to play the tape; (5) if you can't hear the tape when you play it.

Or suppose you just trust to your "will power" or your determination. You may be still less inclined to read this book before you go to sleep. You may forget about it entirely.

On the other hand, you may discover this: You are more inclined to read this book if (1) very often you see several large, colored, bright signs which advise you to read this book for half an hour before you go to bed; (2) if you see this book often, standing on its end and well-lighted; (3) if you play the tape and listen to it morning and night; and (4) if someone gives you a verbal signal occasionally.

Don't take my word for this. Actually make these experiments yourself.

Key No. 3. You Can Start Arcs, And Help Maintain Them, With Visualized Images

When you see an object, a change occurs in your eyes. The result is a visual image. As you remember from the first part of this chapter, this is what you react to when you look at something. You don't react to the object itself.

Ordinarily your visual images are clear and sharp.

Now close your eyes. *Imagine* you are looking at some object. You will have a *visualized* image of the object.

You have often seen a yellow taxicab. *Imagine,* now, that you are looking at one. If your *visualized* image is very clear and sharp it can be almost the same as the *visual* image you have when you actually look at the cab.

How strong can visualized images be?

Steinmetz, the famous electrical engineer and inventor, developed many of his new inventions in his head. He said he could manipulate his visualized images and revise and reshape the apparatus or machine in his thinking. He could "see" the new machine in operation long before he began to make his drawings.

Visualized images can start stimulus-response arcs and incline you toward certain acts. The stronger, clearer, and more often repeated the visualized image is, the more surely will you carry out the act.

Try it for yourself. Start now. At least once every hour between now and tomorrow night, and for a minute or two at a time, visualize yourself reading this book. Put a small piece of adhesive tape on your thumb to remind you.

In your imagination see yourself sitting in a comfortable chair, with a good light, reading this book for half an hour. Make your visualized picture as clear as possible. Try to make it as clear as though you were actually seeing yourself reading the book.

Also tonight, as you go to sleep, visualize yourself reading this book. Do the same as you wake up in the morning. Be sure to do this. It is very important.

Create visualized images throughout the day and as you go to sleep at night. Observe how they help you perform the act. You can soon prove to yourself that your visualized images help start stimulus-response arcs.

Key No. 4. You Can Start Arcs And Help Maintain Them With The Right Inner Speech

An inner speech stimulus is a statement you make to yourself. Examples: You are driving your car along the street when you edge over toward the curb. The stimulus for this act was the words you said to yourself: "I almost forgot! I must pick up the meat at the butcher's." Leaving the butcher's, you drive directly to the post office. The stimulus that brought about this arc (driving to the post office) was your inner speech, "I must get some stamps." Then you stop and buy a magazine. The stimulus was the words you thought, "I wonder what happens in the serial this week?" Arriving home you immediately turn around and go back to town. The inner speech stimulus? You said to yourself, "Goodness gracious (or some more appropriate expression), I forgot to buy Mary her birthday present!"

Your inner speech can start stimulus-response arcs. How can you tell? The arcs show themselves in your acts. The words you say to yourself tend to make you act in certain ways, according to your words.

Try it for yourself. Start now. Between now and tomorrow night say these words to yourself over and over, several times every hour: "Tomorrow night I will read the book, *How To Work Miracles In Your Life,* for half an hour before I go to bed."

Remember, just say these words over and over to yourself throughout the day. A piece of adhesive tape on the palm of your hand will remind you. Also, say the words to yourself as you go to sleep tonight, and as you awaken in the morning. Then see how much you are inclined to read this book tomorrow evening.

Remember! Don't just assume it works. Actually make the experiment. This is very important. You must get the "feel" of these methods.

Key No. 5. You Can Start Arcs And Help Keep Them With Implicit Kinesthetic Movements

Kinesthesis is what we call the sense whose end organs lie in your muscles, tendons, and joints. These end organs are stimulated by your bodily movements. Kinesthesis is known as the "muscle sense."

Open and close your hand. What you feel is the movement of the muscles, tendons, and joints in your hand.

Your muscle movements are of two kinds: (1) Explicit and (2) implicit. Your explicit movements can be seen; your implicit movements are inside you and can't be seen. But any implicit movement creates a stimulus. The stimulus, in turn, brings about a stimulus-response arc inside you.

You can easily experience the effect of your implicit muscular movements. Go where you will not be disturbed. Sit down and relax. Now close your eyes and for five minutes concentrate all your innner or implicit muscle movements on the activity of writing a letter to a certain friend. Without moving, feel yourself writing the letter. Do this for five minutes. Now— do you feel inclined to write the letter? As a matter of fact, you may actually write it!

These implicit kinesthetic movements are important stimuli. They spark stimulus-response arcs. Have the inner muscle movements of walking, and you tend to walk. Have the implicit muscle movements of talking, and you tend to speak.

Now make this experiment: Once an hour sit down and concentrate your implicit muscle movements on the act of reading this book for half an hour before you go to bed. Concentrate in this way for five minutes each time.

Sit where you will not be disturbed. Relax. Then, without moving, *feel* yourself getting settled with the book. Feel your muscles holding the book. Feel your eyes moving. Feel through the complete reading activity.

Also, as you go to sleep tonight, and as you wake up in the morning, be sure to "feel" yourself reading this book.

Do all this and see if you are more inclined to read this book for half an hour before you go to bed.

You have undoubtedly discovered that it's hard to use Key No. 3, 4, or 5 by itself. The other two Keys come into the act automatically.

A logical way to use this tendency is simply to practice all three Keys at the same time.

Select any act you wish to perform. Learn to visualize everything you should see when you perform the act correctly. Learn to say the words to yourself which describe the perfect performance of the act. Learn to feel your muscles, on the implicit level, perform the act correctly. Then, while you are comfortably seated, or even while lying down, and without appearing to move a muscle, put the three activities together. Carry on Key activities Nos. 3, 4, and 5 at the same time.

For example, suppose you want to visit your dentist. You know you should go, but you are in no pain. You have been putting off the visit for a long time. Now you are no more eager to go to the dentist than you were before, but you wish to try this plan.

This is what you do. Sit where you will be comfortable and undisturbed. Say something like this to yourself: "Tomorrow morning at about 10 o'clock I will call my dentist and make an appointment. I will say to the receptionist, 'May I have an appointment for 3 p.m.?'"

In addition, and without moving, *feel* yourself walking to the phone. Feel yourself removing the receiver, dialing your dentist, and asking for the appointment.

At the same time, visualize what you would actually see if you were placing the call. Visualize the phone book, the telephone, the desk, or whatever supports the phone and "see" your watch with the small hand at 10.

In other words, *all at the same time*, and while you remain absolutely still, (1) say the words to yourself which you would say to the receptionist, (2) feel yourself phoning for an appointment, and (3) visualize what you would actually see if you were really making the phone call.

If you are interested in improving any skill, whether in a sport, for use in your vocation, or in connection with your hobby, be sure to use Key procedures 3, 4, and 5 together, as explained above.

If you would like an illustration in the field of sports, see the article by E. F. Wells in the December 1962 issue of *Golf Digest*.

*Key No. 6. You Can Improve The Arcs You Want To Develop
          By Improving Your Physical Condition And Func-
          tioning*

Your general physical condition affects your stimulus-response arcs. When your physical condition is bad, the desired stimulus-response arcs may be interfered with or stopped entirely.

A good example here is the person who has allowed his general physical condition to weaken. His insufficient strength and energy may make it impossible for many desirable arcs to show themselves. His weakness keeps him from doing many things he would like to do or which he wants to do.

Think of a man who becomes desperately ill. His temperature rises to 105 degrees. Will his stimulus-response arcs operate normally? Of course not.

Or suppose a person develops stomach trouble. Then this distressed organ sends its own arcs through his system. The man recognizes them as pain. They interfere with the good arcs he tries to establish.

But the physical condition is not alone in its influence on your behavior. The general functioning of the body must also be considered.

Think of the effect of alcohol. Picture a man driving his automobile expertly. All his stimulus-response arcs operate normally. Now he stops at a bar and has several drinks of whiskey. What happens? His physical functioning is changed. His stimulus-response arcs no longer operate normally. If he drives, he may have a serious accident.

Then there is the person who is usually calm and relaxed. His stimulus-response arcs are normal. But suppose this person becomes fearful, worried, nervous, anxious, full of fright, or filled with dread. What happens? He is filled with adrenaline. This brings about many internal changes. The changes stop or modify the stimulus-response arcs inside him. The actor frozen by stage fright, for instance, can't experience normal stimulus-response arcs.

Finally, consider the very common condition of general muscular tension. When this exists, all the muscles are tense. They can't function normally. If your muscles are tense, every one of your stimulus-response arcs which requires the action of your muscles is interfered with. If you are a ball player and your muscles are tense, you can't play good baseball. That's why the team managers try so hard to keep the ball players relaxed or, as they call it, "loose."

Many stimulus-response arcs operate inside you. Most of these arcs end with some muscle response. Do you want to keep and strengthen your arcs which lead to the right muscle action? Do you want certain good actions? Then be sure to maintain what we might call "active relaxation." This is a condition in which every muscle not needed for the act is relaxed. It's what Dr. Jacobson calls "differential relaxation" in his book, *You Must Relax*.[1]

To help your stimulus-response arcs operate correctly: (1) Improve your general physical condition. (2) Keep yourself in good physical condition.[2] (3) Avoid the use of alcohol or anything else which upsets your physical operation when you want a good arc. (4) Avoid fear and all the negative emotions. (5) Develop active relaxation as a habit.

Key No. 7. You Can Make Good Arcs Stronger By The Proper Use Of Pleasure

When you are awake and alert, you are conscious. Then you are aware of yourself and your surroundings.

This consciousness you experience has a certain content. The sensations in your consciousness may be pleasant or unpleasant.

The pleasant content of your consciousness may be physical

---

[1] Edmund Jacobson, M.D., *You Must Relax* (New York: McGraw-Hill Book Company, Inc., 1957).
[2] See Chapters 6 and 7.

pleasure, as when you eat a good meal after a day's fast. It may be psychological pleasure, as when you make a decision which proves to be exceptionally good.

The unpleasant content of your consciousness may be physical pain, as when you have a toothache. Or it may be the psychological pain which follows an unwise decision.

Is there any relationship between what you experience in consciousness and the operation of your stimulus-response arcs? There is.

This is the law: When you do something which is accompanied or followed by a feeling of pleasure, the stimulus-response arc which brought about the act tends to continue. Also the arc tends to repeat. This means that any time you do something, and the act is accompanied or followed by pleasure, you will be inclined to continue the act and/or to repeat it.

You will think of many examples. Taste a dish of delicious ice cream, or eat a few salted peanuts. The act is accompanied by a feeling of pleasure. You are inclined to taste the ice cream or the salted peanuts again. In fact, you may eat all the ice cream or all the peanuts!

Read a book by a certain author. If you enjoy the book you may read all the other books by the same author.

You tend to repeat any act when it is accompanied by, or followed by, a feeling of pleasure.

Consequently, if you want one of your stimulus-response arcs to continue, or to repeat at a later time, see that the operation of the arc (the act) is accompanied or followed by pleasure.

Let's say that you want to establish the arc of reading this book for half an hour every evening before you go to bed. Then every time you perform the act—every time you read the book for half an hour before you go to bed—give yourself a reward of some kind. You might eat a bit of some food of which you are especially fond. Use the reward to put some pleasure with, or right after, the reading. This helps keep the arc alive.

Key No. 8. You Can Improve The Arcs You Want By Improving The Condition Of Your Nerves And Brain

The impulses from your receptors must travel along the nerves (See Figure 1). So the physical condition of your nerves is important. If your nerve cells are starved, or if your nerves are defective from any other cause, the normal operation of the stimulus-response arc will be interfered with. It will be like defective wires in a telephone system (Figures 4 and 6).

Your brain must also be in good condition. It sorts out the messages which come to it from your receptors. Then it routes the messages to your effectors (Figure 1). The condition of your brain and the quantity and quality of the brain cells is extremely important.

There is also evidence that your brain exercises some control over your glands. Your glands govern your emotions by secreting hormones. If your brain is in poor condition your glands may be affected. They may secrete hormones in the wrong amounts or at the wrong times. The wrong supply of hormones can interfere with the operation of your stimulus-response arcs. Then you may blame your wrong behavior on your emotions and not on your brain, where the blame may really belong.

Your brain differs from the brain of every other person. Some of your brain differences are hereditary. Others are a matter of your nutrition. Also, injuries, concussions, operations, and physical breakdowns in the brain bring about changes in the operation of this organ.

Any one, or a group of factors, can interfere with the correct operation of your brain. Then your brain, in turn, may interfere with the correct operation of your stimulus-response arcs. It works the same as defects in the central machine in the telephone system.

If you can improve the physical condition of your brain, you can improve the operation of your stimulus-response arcs. The result will be the improvement of your behavior.

When you think about reading in this book before you go to

bed tomorrow night, ask yourself this question, "What am I doing to improve the physical condition of my brain?" If your answer is "Nothing," Chapters 6 and 7 should interest you.

Key No. 9. You Can Make Arcs Stronger By Improving Your Receptors

Suppose a person is somewhat deaf. His ears will then pick up fewer auditory signals (words, music, sounds of all kinds). He will experience fewer stimuli and consequently have fewer stimulus-response arcs. Without the right arcs he won't react properly to certain questions, statements, and other sounds. He could fail to hear a warning. He could walk into danger.

Or suppose someone's eyes are defective. Then his eyes will miss many visual signals (signs, warnings, evidence of approaching danger). With fewer effective signals he will have fewer stimuli and fewer stimulus-response arcs. The result may be that he doesn't react to a warning sign and he hurts himself.

What can you do if you want to get more "good" arcs started in you by outside signals? You can improve your receptors. Or you can improve the results you get from certain receptors by using "helpers," such as glasses or a hearing aid.

When you contemplate the reading of this book tomorrow night, give some thought to the condition of your eyes. If you can make your eyes function better, it will be easier for you to read. The easier it is for you to read, the more you will be inclined to read in this book before you go to bed.

Key No. 10. You Can Improve Arcs By Improving Your Effectors

Suppose one of your effectors is damaged. It might be your right hand. Suppose you need that effector to make the right response in a certain situation. You may want to shake hands with a friend. Obviously it will be difficult, or impossible, for the right stimulus-response arc to operate.

You can easily see that your stimulus-response arcs are

greatly influenced by the condition of the effectors involved.

Do you want to improve the operation of a certain stimulus-response arc? Then improve the condition of your effectors which give the response and which make the act possible.

Use the keys all together

Now you have ten Keys. These are things you can do to start, strengthen, and keep the stimulus-response arcs you want. Use these Keys to bring about the acts you wish to perform.

We have discussed the ten Keys one at a time. But this doesn't mean that you must use them one at a time. The more of these factors you use at the same time, the more surely will you get the arc, and consequently the behavior, you desire.

An example

To see how these Keys can be used together to get a certain action, watch a bored employee!

As soon as he starts to work he prepares himself for his one big, important act of the day. This is the dash home at quitting time!

He prepares himself by glancing often at the clock (Key No. 1). The clock is one of his signals.

To supplement this signal, many times every hour he looks at some of the other employees who are loafing (Key No. 2).

He visualizes himself dashing away from work when the 4:30 whistle blows (Key No. 3).

He says to himself often, "Won't it be wonderful when 4:30 comes? Then I can go home!" (Key No. 4).

Almost constantly he "feels" himself punching his time card and running out the door (Key No. 5).

Off the job he carries on a variety of activities which worsen his physical condition (Key No. 6). This makes it hard for him to do his work and easy to think about going home.

He encourages himself to continue this visualizing, thinking and feeling by thinking about all the fun he will have as soon as he gets away from work (Key No. 7).

What is the result? The action for which he so thoroughly prepares himself is almost sure to follow. He dashes home when the whistle blows!

Suppose the boss wants him to stay and work overtime. The employee knows he will be paid time-and-a-half. Does he stay and help his employer? No. He can't. He has prepared himself too well for his run out the gate!

Another example

But you don't have to look only at a bad example. Here's a *good* example. Here's an employee who uses the ten Keys to get himself to carry out the act he wants to perform.

This employee prepares himself for the activity he wants. This is to do this work better than anyone else. He sets himself a production goal, and this becomes one of his signals (Key No. 1).

He sets up other signals.

He observes other excellent workers, and these become additional signals (Key No. 2).

All through the day he visualizes himself turning out an abundance of perfect work (Key No. 3).

He repeats to himself often such words as: "I'm learning fast. I do my work better all the time" (Key No. 4).

Constantly he "feels" himself doing his work fast and well (Key No. 5).

He improves his physical condition and maintains his efficient functioning (Key No. 6).

He increases the pleasure he gets from his work; he rewards himself for good work (Key No. 7).

He encourages himself by thinking about the possible rewards ahead—increased pay, the position of foreman, superintendent, and even president!

He does all he can to keep his nerves, brain, receptors, and effectors in good condition (Keys No. 8, 9, and 10).

Now, if another employee suggests that he stop work and clean up thirty minutes ahead of time, this employee refuses. He says, "I wish I could, but I've got this job to finish. I can just about get it done by quitting time."

This employee can't knock off early because he has prepared himself so well for the efficient action he wants! If the boss wants him to work overtime, he's ready and willing.

To get the most out of life you must establish the right stimulus-response arcs. You must carry on the separate acts which bring you the good things you want.

We have just seen the ten Keys you can use to get yourself to perform any act you select. Use these Keys to make yourself perform the acts you need to get what you want from life.

But it is not enough just to strive for the good things of life. You must also avoid the wrong acts which bring trouble upon you. This is because troubles drain your power. They make it difficult or impossible for you to get the most out of life.

Now let's see how you can avoid the acts which get you into trouble.

SEVEN PROCEDURES TO AVOID STIMULUS-RESPONSE ARCS

(Seven Ways to Keep Yourself from Doing Something)

Procedure A. Eliminate The Signals Which Bring The Wrong Arcs

How can you prevent the formation of the wrong arcs? Get rid of the signals which start them.

Suppose you *should* study for an examination. Instead, you go riding with a friend in his new car. The signal which starts the arc of joy riding is the invitation of your friend. Over and over he says, "Come on. Forget the books. You can study some other time. Come for a ride."

You really want to avoid the joy riding. This means that you must stop the stimulus-response arc which results in the rides. So you stop the signals which trigger the arc. You make your friend be silent. Or you get away from him. Then you eliminate the wrong signal.

Procedure B. Stop The Visualized Images Which Start The Wrong Arcs

We have seen how you can help establish stimulus-response arcs by visualizing the performance of the act. To *avoid* an arc, and consequently to avoid an act, *don't* visualize yourself performing the act.

Let's say that the act you wish to avoid is eating rich desserts. Then you must avoid all visualized images of yourself eating the desserts. Also, avoid all visualized images of the desserts themselves.

Don't conjure up tempting mental pictures of pies, cakes, puddings, crepes suzette, and ice cream sundaes. Instead, the moment such a mental picture appears, switch to some other visualized image. Switch, for example, to a visualized image of yourself slim, healthy, and handsome. Switch to visualized images of yourself sipping a small cup of after-dinner coffee, if you drink coffee. Or "see" yourself eating a small piece of fresh fruit and a piece of cheese.

Procedure C. Stop The Inner Speech Which Starts The Wrong Arc

You learned to promote the performance of an act by "talking yourself into it." You simply talk to yourself about the performance of the act.

Now, to prevent the occurrence of an arc, stop this inner speech activity which starts the arc.

The easiest way to stop the wrong inner speech is to concentrate on the right speech. So when you catch yourself thinking the wrong words, switch to the right words, and concentrate on them.

Suppose you want to avoid the act of smoking cigarettes. Let's say that you stop smoking for a while. Then you begin to think, "Wouldn't a cigarette taste wonderful! I'd give anything to sit down and enjoy a cigarette."

Now you must change your inner speech. You must say words to yourself which describe some other act. A good way to do this is to memorize a statement which describes a substitute act you do wish to perform. In this case you might memorize the following statement and switch to it when you think about smoking! "I realize that smoking is largely a nervous habit. Instead of smoking, I relax. I relax all my muscles as much as I possibly can."

Procedure D. Stop Your Implicit Muscle Movements Which Start The Arc

You remember how you can *start* stimulus-response arcs by repeating implicit muscle movements similar to the overt muscle movements of the act itself.

Now, to avoid an arc you *don't* want, stop the implicit muscle movements which help start the arc.

Suppose you have been playing golf for many years. Now, for some good reason, you wish to avoid the act. When you begin to "feel" yourself playing golf, change your implicit muscle movements to those for some other activity you enjoy. "Feel" yourself walking through the countryside, for example. Or "feel" yourself bowling on the green.

Procedure E. Remove Or Minimize The Pleasure Which Comes With The Act. Increase The Pain

Consider an act you would like to avoid. Can you decrease or eliminate the pleasure which normally comes with the act? Do this and you will be less inclined to perform the act.

Suppose, for example, that you like to play bridge. Now, for some reason, you wish to stop playing. Then play with uncongenial partners in unsatisfactory surroundings. You will be less inclined to play.

Increase the pain which accompanies an act and it helps you avoid the act. Consider the act of smoking. Suppose you want to avoid this act. Can you do something to make the cigarette taste bad? If you can, you will be less inclined to smoke.

A good way to increase the pain which accompanies an act is to set up penalties. Fine yourself. Punish yourself. If you indulge in the act give something valuable to someone you don't like.

Procedure F. Think About The Bad Consequences Of The Act

To avoid an act, concentrate on the painful or unsatisfactory consequences.

Let us say that you have been warned by your doctor that you must reduce your weight by 50 pounds to avoid heart trouble. This means that you must eat about half the amount you are used to. How can you make it easier to avoid eating the extra 1,500 calories of food you are accustomed to? Think, most of the time, about the bad consequences of overeating. Say words to yourself about the dangers of overeating. In your thinking, associate a poor appearance, pain, weakness, illness, and possibly death with the overeating. This will help you avoid the act you don't want.

Think about the penalties when you think of an act you wish to stop. Think more about the penalties than you do about the act. This helps you avoid the act.

Procedure G. Improve Your Physical Condition

Many acts you may wish to avoid are made easier by a poor physical condition. Consider drinking, for example. It's easier to drink when you are ill, nervous, fatigued, or upset.

Suppose you want to avoid this act. Then improve your physical condition. This will make it easier for you to avoid the wrong behavior.

Consider the act of smoking. All other things being normal, the worse your physical condition the easier it is to smoke. The better your physical condition, the easier it is to avoid the act. If you want to avoid the act of smoking, improve your physical condition (Chapters 6 and 7).

Think of any act which is encouraged by a poor physical

condition. Improve your physical condition and it will be easier to avoid the act.

To avoid an act, use all the procedures at the same time

Let's say that you are very fond of Shakespeare. A famous actor is to do Richard III on TV tomorrow night. You are eager to see the show. But, for some reason you have decided not to see it. We shall assume that watching the show will get you into some sort of trouble. Here's how you can use the seven Procedures to help you avoid the act you wish to avoid.

A. Get rid of the signals. Put all notices of the show out of sight. Avoid conversations about the show. Put the TV out of sight, too, or avoid the room where the TV is kept. B. Avoid or stop all visual images of yourself watching the show. Form visualized images of other activities. C. Stop all your inner speech about watching the show. Think, in terms of words, about other activities. D. Stop any implicit muscle movements having to do with watching the show. Have implicit muscle movements of other activities. E. Plan, should you watch the show, to throw the TV image somewhat out of focus. Plan to wear tight shoes and uncomfortable clothes. F. Think about the bad consequences of watching the TV. There must be some bad consequences or you would not have decided against it. Also, establish some punishment for yourself should you watch the show. G. Improve your physical condition. Be so full of vim and energy that the thought of sitting still in a darkened room is unpleasant.

Instructions if you have not yet learned the 18 steps of the decision-making technique

You have learned the ten Keys. These help you perform any act. Use as many of the ten Keys as you need to get yourself to memorize the 18 Steps of the Decision-Making Technique.

Then use the Decision-Making Technique with every important decision you make.

While you use the Decision-Making Technique with your current decisions, read Chapter 5. In that chapter you will learn about the proposed plan to help you get the most out of life.

Chapter 5

LET YOUR HABITS BRING YOU THE GOOD
THINGS OF LIFE

In this chapter you learn how to establish
all the good, new habits *you need to get
the most out of life. You also learn how
to* stop *your* wrong habits, *which keep
you* away *from the good things of life.*

"Whenever you are angry, be assured that it is not only a
present evil, but that you have increased a habit, and added
fuel to a fire."

Those are the words of Epictetus, the famous Greek philosopher.

What he says, of course, is true. But Epictetus could have
said the same about *anything* you do which is wrong. When
you do *anything* you shouldn't do you may either start or
strengthen a bad habit.

About 1800 years after Epictetus came the British natural
philosopher, John Tyndall. He said, "The formation of right
habits is essential to your permanent security. They diminish
your chances of failing when assailed, and they augment your
chances of recovery when overthrown."

We could paraphrase this and say, "The formation of right
habits is essential to your security and peace of mind. They

lessen your chances of getting into trouble. If you do get into trouble, they help you get out."

Then only a little later came our own American novelist and humorist, Mark Twain. He said, "Habit is habit, and not to be flung out of the window by any man, but coaxed downstairs a step at a time."

Are you ready for the plan?

In the last chapter you learned some of the important facts in the field of human behavior. You will remember, however, that in that chapter we considered only the performance or the avoidance of single acts. There was no discussion of the formation of habits.

Now you should be ready for the plan.

Actually, there are two plans. The first has to do with the development of the good new habits you need. The second plan shows you how to stop your bad habits.

The first plan enables you to coax the good new habits "upstairs."

The second plan makes it possible to coax your bad habits "downstairs a step at a time."

At this time, remember, you are to make no decision. Do not accept or reject the plans as you read them. Simply read the plans given below. Then, after you know all about each plan, use the 18 Steps and make your wise decision.

THE FIRST PLAN—ESTABLISH GOOD NEW HABITS

What Is A Habit?

A habit is a succession of single acts which follow each other rather automatically.

The habit of making wise decisions is just one careful use of the Decision-Making Technique repeated automatically whenever a decision is called for.

The habit of playing good golf is just one good golf swing repeated again and again with certain minor adjustments.

The habit of getting good grades in school is the achievement of one good grade followed by the constant repetition of the same act—getting a good grade.

Select Your First Good New Habit To Add

The purpose of this book is to help you get the most out of life. Logically, then, the first new habit you should add should be one which will help you get something you want. Better still, select a habit which will help you get *many* of the good things of life.

Here's a way to select a good habit to add: Think of something you want from life. Then see what habit will help you get it. Suppose you want more money. What habit can you add which will help you earn more money?

Still another way to select a good habit to add is to watch for suggestions. Someone may suggest a habit which will help you get something you want from life.

But however you do it, right now select one good new habit you should establish.

How To Establish A Good New Habit

First. Determine the exact *act* you want to repeat as a habit.

Second. Learn what you must do to perform the act correctly.

Someone may tell you how to do it. You may read the instructions in a book. You may watch someone do it. You may use all three of these procedures.

Third. Remember exactly what you are to do.

You must be able to close your eyes and *visualize* yourself performing the act correctly. You must be able to *say the words to yourself* which describe the correct performance of the act. Finally, you must, without moving, be able to *feel* your way through the correct performance of the act.

Fourth. Get what you have learned into your muscles. Transfer what you *know* into what you *do*.

Use as many of the Keys from Chapter 4 as you need to get yourself to perform the act once.

Fifth. Use as many of the ten Keys as you need to get yourself to perform the act again and again.

When you have repeated the act often enough, and with a
reasonable amount of pleasure, you have the habit.

An Example

Suppose you ask your employer for a suggestion. He says,
"What you need is the habit of getting here on time every
morning." This is the good new habit you select.

First. The act which must repeat itself is "reaching your
work place at least five minutes before starting time."

Second. You learn how to perform this act correctly. You must
get up at 6:30, leave home at 7:30, connect with your trans-
portation at 7:45, and walk into your place of employment by
8:50.

Third. Visualize everything you plan to do, from getting up
at 6:30 to walking into your place of employment by 8:50.
Describe all these acts to yourself in your *inner speech.* Without moving, *feel* yourself performing all the required acts.

Fourth. Use as many of the ten Keys in Chapter 4 as you
need, to cause yourself to perform the four activities which
make up the habit.

Fifth. Continue your use of the Keys until the habit is established. Then every morning you reach your place of work on
time, and you do it by habit.

If You Suddenly Found Yourself With Five New Habits

Now you have the proposed plan for the development of
your good new habits.

Think how much better off you would be if you suddenly
found yourself with five good new habits of great importance
in your life.

You could have prompt action instead of procrastination.
You could have the habit of saying "No thank you" and refusing to smoke instead of the cigarette habit. You could have
the habit of using your spare time profitably. Or you might
have such habits as a good and dependable golf swing, the

habit of swimming fast and gracefully, the habit of speaking
easily and effectively in public, or the habit of pronouncing
and enunciating your words correctly. Pick any five good new
habits you wish. Wouldn't it be wonderful if you suddenly
found yourself with these new habits?

You Can Have All The New Habits You Wish

Now imagine what it would be like to wake up some morning with not five, but *ten* good new habits. The ten good habits
you need most! That would be wonderful, too. But think of
this: Use the methods given in this book. Go about it correctly
and systematically. In the next few years you can add at least
twenty new habits you want and need most! That's in only a
few years. But you have your whole lifetime ahead of you!
Think how much you can improve yourself in the rest of your
life. Think what you can accomplish! Think how much happier
you will be!

What If It Doesn't Work?

You have studied the ten simple Keys you should follow to
set up a good new habit. It sounds easy, doesn't it? Possibly
you think, "I shall follow the instructions in this chapter. Soon
I'll have every good habit I want."

Then you remember the good habits you have tried to establish in the past. In some cases you failed. You may wonder if
it's really going to be so easy.

Here's exactly what you should do if you make a good effort
and you still don't get the habit you want. Answer these questions and follow these suggestions:

1. Remember Chapter 4. Are your nerve cells and your brain
cells in good condition? You can determine this, partly at least,
by your general physical condition and by the way you react
to normal situations. A good doctor may be able to tell you the
condition of your nerve and brain cells.

2. Are your receptors, which you need for the act which
makes up the habit, in good condition? If not, can you improve
them?

3. Are the effectors you need for the act in good condition?

4. Did you actually set up plenty of signals? Are they all around you? Are you aware of them almost all the time? Do your signals direct you toward the act you want to perform as a habit?

5. Are your visual signals sufficiently large, well-lighted, and brightly colored? Are the auditory signals loud enough?

6. Are there other signals in your environment which set up stimulus-response arcs which are contrary to those of the act you wish to establish? For example, does someone in your family urge you to play some game just before you go to bed, instead of reading this book? If so, get rid of the signals or avoid them.

7. Do you know enough about the act you wish to set up as a habit? Can you close your eyes and "see" yourself, very clearly, performing every step of the act? If not, study the act. Observe some expert as he does what you plan to do. Watch his moves and remember everything. Study diagrams, pictures, and descriptions of the act. Be sure you can visualize it easily.

8. All through the day, at odds moments, do you visualize yourself performing the act you wish to set up as a habit? If not, you may wish to devote ten or fifteen minutes every day as follows: Sit where you will be quiet and undisturbed. Sit upright but relaxed. Close your eyes. Concentrate your visualized images on the act you wish to perform. During the full practice time, "see" yourself performing the act.

Also visualize in this way as you go to sleep and as you wake up in the morning.

9. Do *contrary* visualized images occur? These may be visualized images of yourself performing some other act instead of the one you wish.

For example, suppose that half the time you have the right visualized images of yourself reading this book. The rest of the time you have visualized images of yourself reading a detective story, which is what you have always done just before going to bed. The detective story images come along as a matter of habit. Now you have a contest between the two sets of visualized images. If you want the detective story reading to lose and the reading of this book to win, you must help the arcs you want. You must set up more signals to help you "see" yourself reading this book. You must remove more of the signals which cause you to "see" yourself reading the detective story.

You can also help the arcs you want if you will do this: When you notice a visualized image of yourself doing what you don't want to do—in this case reading the detective story—immediately change it to a visualized image of yourself doing what you *should* do. In this example it is reading this book.

Practice helps. Think of some act you like, but which you know you should not carry out. Call it act A. Think of an act you don't like, but which you know you *should* perform *instead* of act A. Call it act B. Now have a visualized image of yourself performing act A. Hold the image just a second. Then switch and "see" yourself performing act B for a minute or two.

Do this exercise over and over. See if you can't get to the point where you always, and automatically, drop the visualized images of act A at the end of a second, and then view the visualized images of act B for at least a minute.

Remember that your visualized images are simply imagined pictures brought about by muscles in your eyes. Nothing more. Your eyes make the pictures. The act of visualizing is muscular behavior, just as is throwing a ball or biting into an apple. You can learn to control your visual images just as you can learn to control any overt act.

10. Can you describe the act, in words, to another person? Can you make your verbal description so clear that the other person could perform the act correctly? If not, study the act. Learn to describe every step. Be able to recite the steps in the proper order. Practice giving instructions for the performance of the act. Give your instructions aloud, possibly to your reflec-

tion in a mirror. Say, "First I do this. . . . Then I do this. . . ."
Describe every step very carefully.

11. All through the day, whenever your attention is not required elsewhere, do you say over and over to yourself such
words as, "Every day, at ten o'clock (or whatever time you
select) I _____" and describe the act? In our illustration you
might say, "Every evening, just before I go to bed, I get the
book, *How To Work Miracles In Your Life.* I take it to my
chair where I have a good light. I get settled and I read the
book for half an hour. I make notes when I should. I concentrate well and I remember what I read."

If, right now, you don't actually repeat such words to yourself during the day for the act you wish to establish, try this
exercise: Every day, assume a comfortable but upright seated
position. Then for five minutes repeat the words to yourself
which describe the act you wish to perform. This will help you
carry on the same inner speech activity throughout the day.

Use this same inner speech as you go to sleep at night and
as you awaken in the morning.

12. Does contrary inner speech appear often? At various
times through the day do you say words to yourself which
spark an act which interferes with the one you wish to perform?

In our illustration, many times throughout the day you might
find yourself saying these words to yourself, "I wonder what's
going to happen next in my detective story. Just before I go to
bed I'll read the detective story and find out."

In such a case you should increase the number of your signals
which make you think of reading this book. Also decrease the
number of signals which make you think of reading the detective story.

Possibly the best procedure is this exercise: Compose and
learn a statement which says just what you want to do. In our
example you might have the statement, "Every evening I read

for 30 minutes in *How To Work Miracles In Your Life* just before I go to bed."

Learn the statement. Say it over and over to yourself until it comes automatically. Then do this: Every time you catch yourself saying words about the activity you don't want to perform, immediately repeat your formula. Say it over to yourself several times.

Remember, when you think verbally you are just manipulating words. You are simply using your vocal muscles. They're under your complete control. Whenever words come along which you don't want, change them, constantly and patiently, to the words you want. Control your inner speech. Don't let it control you!

13. Can you sit still and "feel" yourself perform the desired act? If not, you may need to carry on the act a few times under supervision. This is to be sure you do it correctly. As you perform the act, give special attention to the feel in your muscles. Then, without moving, you should be able to experience the same feelings.

14. Do you actually feel yourself performing the act many times during the day? If not, every day, for five minutes, assume a comfortable position and *feel* yourself performing the act, but without moving. Also, feel yourself performing the act as you go to sleep and as you wake up in the morning.

Remember that you're the boss! It's up to you to govern your implicit kinesthetic movements and to keep them from ruling you.

15. Is your total physical functioning sound and efficient?

Is your physical condition good? If not, get it right as soon as possible. You need a good, sound physical condition for good arcs. See Chapters 6 and 7.

Do you do anything, or eat, drink, smoke, or take anything, which upsets your stimulus-response arcs? Especially, do you do this just before, or when, you wish to perform the act? If so, you can't expect to get the habit established. You need to help out the arcs with the most efficient and the best-operating physical condition possible.

Are you sufficiently calm and relaxed? Remember, if your muscles are tense, you'll find it harder to set up a habit you desire. If you are habitually tense, or if you are tense when you wish to perform the act, use the ten Keys in Chapter 4 and establish the habit of calmness and relaxation.

Do you experience any negative emotion at the time you wish to perform the act? Are you worried about something? Frightened? Apprenhensive? If so, you must get rid of these negative emotions. They make it much harder to set up a new act and to establish a habit. Use the ten Keys to set up the right habit—the habit of relaxing.

Do you experience any pain or physical malfunctioning which acts as a stimulus to send its own arcs through your system? If so, these arcs may interfere with the arcs you wish to establish. The pain or the defective part may make it difficult, or even impossible, for you to set up the habit you wish.

If you have any such pain or defect, by all means do all you can to eliminate it.

16. Did you actually do something special to make yourself enjoy the act? Some people are inclined to look on this as "kid stuff." Don't be one of these people. Be sure to do something, or many things, which will give you pleasure as you perform the act, or immediately thereafter. Even gold stars on a chart are helpful.

It's important to think about this, too: When do you experience the greatest pleasure—when you think about an act you enjoy very much, or when you think about an act you hate? Obviously, if you enjoy dancing, you experience pleasure when you have visualized images of yourself dancing, when you say words to yourself about dancing, and when you have implicit muscular movements of yourself dancing. This pleasure will cause you to continue to think about dancing. Also, if you hate to answer letters, you will experience a certain amount of pain when you have visual images of yourself writing a letter, when you say words to yourself about answering letters, and when you feel yourself answering a letter. This pain will cause the thoughts about letter-answering to stop.

Your course of action is clear. If you want any visual images, inner speech, or implicit kinesthetic movements to continue, they must be accompanied or followed by a feeling of pleasure.

If you don't like to answer letters, how can you accompany your thoughts about this act with pleasure? Think about how good you will feel when the letters are answered. Think how glad the other people will be to receive your letters. Can you get some special note paper or a new pen or typewriter? If so, when you think about using these new items you may experience more pleasure.

If you don't care very much about reading this book before you go to bed, how can you add pleasure to your thoughts about reading it? Think about the rewards which will come to you (1) when you make only wise decisions, (2) when you always do exactly the right thing at the right time, by habit, (3) when you enjoy a perfect, or near-perfect physical condition, (4) when you use your spare time efficiently, and (5) when you have plenty of money which you handle wisely.

Always, when you want to get yourself to carry on some activity, think about all the possible rewards.

17. Follow the instruction above. If you still find it difficult to establish the good new habit, you want, remember the Consulting Psychologist. Find one who is well trained, and who subscribes to the ideas presented in this book. He should be able to help you establish the new habit. This will be true, especially, if he uses hypnosis or suggestion given in the hypnoidal state.

A Summary Of The Items In The Check List

We can summarize the items on this check list as follows: Get the best possible physical condition. Continue to improve your physical condition. Then concentrate on Keys No. 1, 2, 3, 4, 5, 6, and 7, in Chapter 4. If you are normal physically, and if you use these seven Keys correctly, you should establish *any* good habit you wish and *as many* good new habits as you desire.

Now you have the complete plan for the development of good, new habits. Will you build all the good new habits you need? Or will you reject the plan?

Use The 18 Steps

Step 1. It is proposed that you develop good new habits. What is the situation which calls for this proposal?

a. Until you have the good new habits you need, you may be forced to refuse many good plans. One of these plans you must refuse may be the one which would bring you the health, fame, or fortune you desire.

b. Presumably, you don't yet have everything you want from life. This tells you that you should establish the good new habits which will help bring you what you want from life.

c. Occasionally you may get into trouble of some kind. Any time you experience a setback, disappointment, hardship, physical pain, or any kind of loss, failure, defeat, or embarrassment you are in trouble. Any trouble tells you to establish the right habits and avoid the trouble in the future.

d. The more trouble in your life, the less time, energy, and money you have. The fewer troubles you experience, the more time, energy, and money you can use to get what you want from life. So any ambition you have also tells you to use this plan and establish the good habits you need.

e. If you are chronically weak, ill, poor, in pain, unhappy, neglected, ignored, pushed around, or in any way deficient, your situation begs you to accept the plan and to improve your condition through the improvement of your habits.

Step 2. The plan is to use the ten Keys and establish a variety of good new habits.

Step 3. The goal of the plan is, first, to enable you to make better and wiser decisions; second, to enable you to keep yourself out of more trouble; third, to help you get what you want out of life; fourth, to give you a good personal adjustment and complete happiness.

Step 4. Look at your list of private goals. Does this proposed plan conflict with any of your personal goals?

Step 5. In this step you need the important facts in the general field of human behavior. You got them in Chapter 4.

Step 6. Is your physical condition right for this plan? If not, you certainly should make it right. See Chapters 6 and 7.

Step 7. Do you have enough control of the operation of the plan? Yes. You have full control.

Steps 8, 9, and 10. Are your mental, emotional, and physical habits right for this plan? Consider them carefully and reach your conclusion. If any of your habits are wrong for this plan be sure to improve them.

Step 11. Is your environment right for the plan? Would your environment make it impossible or difficult for you to develop a variety of good new habits? If so, change your environment.

Step 12. What are the rewards if the plan is successful? What do you think you could accomplish if you had 20 or 30 good new habits?

Step 13. What are the penalties if the plan fails? Not much loss. Only some time and effort.

Step 14. What are the odds in favor of the success of the plan? Follow the simple instructions and the odds should be at least 100 to 1 in favor of success.

Step 15. What will the other fellow do? Would anyone object if you develop an abundance of good habits?

Steps 16 and 17. Can you find a better plan through which to reach the goals of this plan?

Step 18. Now go off by yourself and make your decision. Will you use the plan and develop an abundance of good habits? Will you say "No" to the plan? Take plenty of time and make a wise decision.

Some Suggestions

A. What to do if you decided against the plan.

Did you decide *not* to establish any new habit which will help you get more out of life? If so, forget this plan and start reading again. Learn all about the second plan.

B. What to do if you decided in favor of the plan.

Did you decide to establish some new habits which will help you get more out of life? If so, add one good, new habit. Just now don't read any further! You can't do everything at once. Nothing is more important than learning to establish good, new habits. Build your good, new habit now.

C. When you have established one good, new habit, continue your reading. Learn the second plan.

D. What to do if, after a reasonable time, you haven't established a good, new habit.

Did you decide to add a good new habit? But, after a few days, had you made no start? Then proceed as follows: Return to Chapter 4. Study again the ten Keys. Then actually use enough of the Keys to make yourself perform a desirable act.

Next, follow the instructions for the establishment of a new habit, given in this chapter, and make the act a habit.

E. When you have established one new habit, study the second plan.

THE SECOND PLAN—GET RID OF YOUR OLD BAD HABITS

It is easy to set up a new habit. Just follow the instructions given above.

Ordinarily it is also easy to stop a bad habit.

What Is A Bad Habit?

A bad habit is the automatic repetition of a single act which, for some reason, should *not* be performed.

The chain-smoking cigarette habit is a succession of single puffs. Each puff follows the one before like elephants marching in the circus, each holding the tail of the one ahead. The liquor habit is a succession of single swallows, each following the one before like water over a falls. The bad habit of making snap decisions is simply one single act (a snap decision) repeated automatically whenever a decision is called for.

How To Stop A Bad Habit

First. Select a habit you should stop. If you can't think of one, ask any relative for a suggestion. Ask your employer. Ask a close friend.

Second. Determine the act which is repeated to form the bad habit.

Third. List all the disadvantages of the act which, repeated often, makes up the bad habit.

Fourth. Use the seven Procedures, starting on page 81 of Chapter 4. Use them until any tendency to perform the act is greatly weakened or eliminated entirely.

Fifth. Find a single act which is good (one you want) to put in place of the act you wish to avoid. This will be an act of such a nature that when it is performed, the unwanted act of the bad habit is excluded automatically. For example, suppose you get very angry at the slightest provocation. The bad act is to get red in the face, shout and flash fire from your eyes. The act you should perform in its place is to relax. When you perform this act you prevent, automatically, the acts which show your anger.

Sixth. Go back to the heading, *How to Establish a Good New Habit,* in this chapter. Follow the instructions. Get yourself to perform the substitute act (the desired act) by habit.

It is important to practice Keys No. 3, 4, and 5 often. Practice them constantly throughout the day. Also use these Keys as you go to sleep and as you wake up in the morning. For all of this you may need a reminder. Here are some suggestions:

If you don't wear a ring, get one and wear it. If you wear a ring already, change it to another finger. You will notice it often throughout the day. When you see or feel it, respond by *"seeing"* yourself performing your selected act. Respond by *saying* to yourself, "Oh, yes. I must do such and such." React also by *feeling* yourself performing the act.

Here's another good signal for this purpose: Get a wrist watch and wear it. If you wear one already, change it to your other wrist. Or, if you are a man, put your keys or change in a different pocket. Often you will notice the wrong location of the item. It will be your signal to visualize, to carry on your inner speech, and to feel yourself performing the desired act. *How To Stop The Bad Habit Of Procrastinating—An Illustration Of The Method*

A. When The Act Should Be Done Now.

1. The habit you wish to stop, we shall say, is the habit of postponing some activity you should perform now.

2. What is the act which, repeated, makes up the bad habit of procrastination? It is the act of looking at something which should be done *now*, and scheduling the act for performance at a later time.

3. List the disadvantages which come from procrastination.

First, if you always procrastinate, you never get anything done. Second, even if you procrastinate only at certain times, with certain activities, you greatly decrease your efficiency and effectiveness. Third, your procrastination may interfere with the activities and routines of other people. Fourth, you become known as a less efficient, and possibly an undependable, person. Fifth, your procrastination bothers you. Your unhappy feelings about the bad habit contribute to your feelings of inferiority. Sixth, your procrastination often causes you inconvenience or it requires you to do extra work.

4. Use the seven Procedures from Chapter 4. Use them to weaken the undesired act of looking at something which should be done *now* and scheduling it for performance at a later date.

5. Find a single act which you can substitute for the act of scheduling a "do it now" act for a later date.

Obviously, the substitute act is to do it *now*. "Doing it now" is the act you put in place of the act of "putting it off."

6. Follow the instructions under the heading, *How to Establish a Good New Habit.* Set up the act of "doing it now" as a habit.

As a concrete example, let's say that you hate to write letters. When you receive a letter which calls for an immediate answer, you put it off and put it off. Here's how to stop this bad habit.

1. The habit you wish to stop is the habit of putting off the answer to a letter which should be answered right now.

2. The bad act you repeat is this: You look at the letter which should be answered *now*, and you make a vague plan to answer it later.

3. The disadvantages which come with the procrastination are given above.

4. Use the seven Procedures from Chapter 4. Weaken the act of putting off the answer.

5. The single act you plan to perform is the immediate reply to any letter which should be answered as soon as received.

6. Use the instructions under *How to Establish a Good New Habit.* Establish the habit of answering immediately every letter which should have a prompt answer.

B. When The Act Should Be Performed Later On.

There is another procrastination habit you might like to stop.

Suppose you contemplate something which *should* be done later on. You think, "I'll do it in a week or two."

The next time something reminds you of the act you say to yourself, "I don't feel like doing it now. There's no hurry. I'll put it off for a while."

Then what? You may never get it done. As a result, you may find yourself in trouble.

Now what should you do? Use the six suggestions under *How to Stop A Bad Habit.*

First. The habit you wish to stop is the habit of postponing an act indefinitely.

Second. The repeated act is scheduling the act for performance at some *indefinite* future time which never comes.

Third. List the disadvantages.

Fourth. Use the seven Procedures until your tendency to postpone an act indefinitely is weakened.

Fifth. The activity you can put in place of the procastination is this: Decide exactly *when* you will perform the act. Pick a time. Enter the date and time on your calendar. Look at your calendar every morning. When the time comes for the performance of the act, *do it now!*

Sixth. Use the suggestions under *How to Establish a Good New Habit.* Cause yourself to carry on the activity you selected to put in place of the procrastination.

The Whole Routine In A Nut Shell

Now let's combine the procedures.

Some act is suggested, or it suggests itself, for performance. First, decide whether or not you will perform the act at all. Second, if you decide that the act *should* be performed, decide when you should do it—*now,* or *later on.* Third, if the act should be performed at once, use enough of the ten Keys and cause yourself to do it *now.* Fourth, if the act should be performed later on, decide exactly *when* you will do it. Pick a definite time. Fifth, use enough of the ten Keys to get yourself to enter the date and time on your calendar. Sixth, use enough of the ten Keys to get yourself to look at your calendar every morning. Seventh, when the date and time come for the performance of the act, use enough of the ten Keys to get yourself to perform the act at once, which is then *now.*

The Whole Routine And The Dentist

Let's say that one of your teeth develops a rough edge.

First, decide whether or not you will see your dentist. Second, if you decide to go to the dentist, decide when. Third, if you decide that you should got at once, use the ten Keys and cause yourself to go to the dentist *now.* Fourth, if you decide that you should go later on, decide exactly when you will phone for an appointment. Fifth, use the ten Keys and get yourself to enter the time and date on your calendar. Sixth, use the ten Keys to cause yourself to look at your calendar every morning.

Seventh, when the date and time come to see the dentist, use the ten Keys and phone for an appointment. Then, if necessary, use the ten Keys to get yourself to go to the dentist at the appointed time.

Can you imagine what your life will be like when you *never* procrastinate?

A Suggested Exercise

Select a few actions you have been postponing for some time. For example, for a long time have you been thinking that you should have your will redrawn? Should you visit your doctor for a checkup? Should you bring your life insurance—and your other insurance too—up to date? Should you refurbish or repair some part of your home? Should you write a certain letter? Should you read a recommended book? Have you been postponing some of these activities? Can you think of other activities you have been putting off for a long time? If you have, here is the exercise: Select an act you have been postponing for a long time. Use the suggestions in this chapter. See if you stop the procrastinating. See if you get it done!

Your First Ace In The Hole

Sometimes it isn't easy to weaken a bad habit and to get the good new habit started. This may be because you don't understand the bad habit. You don't know exactly what it is. You don't know why it means so much to you. When this is true it often helps to learn just what the bad habit is and why you are so fond of it.

In other cases your bad habit may be a complicated affair. You can't figure out exactly what good habit you should put in its place.

There is no room here for a discussion of all the possible bad habits. Fortunately this isn't necessary. All you have to do is read *How to Make and Break Habits*,[1] by James L. Mursell. He discusses most of the usual bad habits.

If you have a habit problem, read the book carefully. You

---

[1] (J. B. Lippincott Company, 1953).

will enjoy the many case histories and interesting illustrations.

The book will also give you a further insight into the way you operate. If you have any trouble stopping a bad habit and starting a new habit, Dr. Mursell's book should help you.

Suppose, for instance, that you want to get rid of the habit of "blowing your top." Look in the index of Dr. Mursell's book under "anger." In the text you will find a discussion of the problem and suggested good habits to establish in place of the anger. Then use the suggestions in this chapter and establish the good habits you should have.

If you wish to establish the habit of saying "No thank you" when urged to smoke a cigarette, see the book, *How to Stop Smoking*,[2] by Herbert Brean.

If you want to set up the habit of saying, "Thank you, no. I'm on the wagon," and the habit of refusing to drink alcoholic beverages, be sure to read the book, *Nutrition and Alcoholism*,[3] by Roger J. Williams.

Also, if you would like to stop smoking, drinking, or overeating, be sure to pay special attention to Chapters 6 and 7.

Your Second Ace In The Hole

Suppose you find it difficult to weaken the wrong act. Suppose this makes it difficult to establish the good substitute act as a habit. Then remmeber the well-trained consulting psychologist. He will have the methods of the professional. One of these should be hypnosis. Or he might use suggestion in the hypnoidal state. Add his methods to those you learn here and you should eliminate any bad habit.

Make Your Wise Decision

You have now learned the second plan. This plan proposes that you get rid of all your habits which get you into trouble. It is proposed that you eliminate all your habits which keep you from getting the most out of life. It is further proposed that you put good habits in their place.

---

[2] (Vanguard, 1958).
[3] (University of Oklahoma Press, 1951).

The goal of the plan is your personal improvement to such a point that you keep yourself out of all trouble while you get what you want out of life.

Will you use the plan and get rid of all your bad habits? Use the 18 Steps of the Decision-Making Technique and make your wise decision.

The suggestions

A. You have now used the 18 Step Decision-Making Technique. You have made your wise decision. Did you decide *not* to get rid of any of your habits which get you into trouble? Then go right on to Chapter 6.

B. Did you decide *to* get rid of at least one bad habit? If so, start right now and eliminate the bad habit. Don't read ahead until you do this. The rest of the book will wait. First get rid of the bad habit.

C. When you have gotten rid of one bad habit, answer these questions:

Do you think it is important, right now, to get rid of more bad habits?

Do you think it is important to build more good habits?

If so, stay with this chapter for a while. Get the habits you need to get the most out of life. Eliminate more of the habits that get you into trouble.

On the other hand, do you think it is more important to develop yourself in other ways? Then continue with your reading. The next chapter is waiting for you.

Chapter 6

ONCE THERE WAS A LITTLE CELL

In this chapter you learn the important facts about you and your physical condition. You lay the foundation for the creation of the physical energy you need to get the most out of life.

It is reported that, for most of his adult life, Mr. Godfrey Lowell Cabot got up at 7 a.m. He took a cold shower, dressed, and ate his breakfast. Then he walked the four or five miles to his office and back again in the evening. He neither drank nor smoked. At 72 he could beat opponents half his age at tennis. He died in his sleep at 101.

Most people are more like the man in a ballad which they sang in the early days on the Mexican border:

> Oh, I eat when I'm hungry,
> I drink when I'm dry,
> And if liquor don't kill me
> I'll live 'till I die.

Or they may agree with Bismark when he said, "No man has lived until he has smoked 100,000 cigars and drunk 10,000 bottles of wine."

You have your own attitude toward the above activities. But no matter what your attitudes may be, we can be sure of this: Your ability to get the most out of life depends on your *power*.

Much of your power comes from your physical energy. Develop a fine, steady flow of physical energy and you will have much of the miraculous power you need to get the most out of life.

Unfortunately, simply to develop physical energy is not enough. You must also avoid the *loss* of energy. Most of this loss comes as the result of physical troubles. Physical troubles weaken you. They sap your energy. They keep you from getting the most out of life.

A physical trouble, of course, is any ailment, disease, weakness, pain, deterioration, allergy, sickness, or infection.

When there is anything wrong with you physically you experience a loss of energy. To preserve your energy you must avoid all physical troubles.

Notice now that the present idea is to *keep* yourself out of physical trouble. It is not to *get* yourself out of trouble. The assumption is that your doctor will get you out of any health trouble you may have. But here's something interesting: Do what is necessary to *keep* yourself out of physical trouble. Then automatically you improve your physical condition. You develop more power.

The suggestion is twofold. First, develop a strong, steady flow of physical energy. Second, prevent the loss of your energy by avoiding all physical troubles.

Your reaction will not be a snap decision, of course. You will get enough facts in the general field of the plan. You will study the plan. You will then use the 18 Step Decision-Making Technique and make a wise decision.

How to get the facts

You have, already, many facts in this general field of health and physical fitness. You have gathered them in the course of your living. It is possible, however, that you could use some additional facts. Or you may wish to check some of the facts you have now.

This is a field in which there is much conflict of opinion. It isn't easy to sift the wheat of truth from the chaff of crazy notions, personal opinions, irresponsible statements, and commercial propaganda. It isn't easy to see what is fact and what is fiction.

It is possible, just the same, to get the facts. You have only to study the books written by the experts and to consult with the experts themselves.

When you have all the important facts you will be ready to consider the plan. Then you can make your wise decision.

Start with the well-known fact that a chain is no stronger than its weakest link. You, also, are no stronger than *your* weakest link. What are your "links"? They are your cells. These are the units of your physiological structure.

You, therefore, are no stronger than your weakest *cell*.

When you were just one cell

Now you are big and made up of millions of cells. But about nine months before you were born you were just *one* cell. At that time you were round and only about 1/200ths of an inch in diameter!

Think of that! That was *you*! 1/200ths of an inch! You were not just small. You were microscopic!

But it's still more amazing that even when you were one cell and microscopic in size, inside you were about 50,000 genes! The genes came in the two cells which united to become you. Half the genes came from your mother (affected by her ancestors), and half your genes came from your father (also influenced by his ancestors).

Can you imagine yourself 1/200ths of an inch in diameter, with 50,000 genes inside?

These genes had much to say about how you developed from the one cell to the time of your birth. You grew from one cell to two, from two to four, and so on. Your genes, in each cell, caused you to develop as a boy or girl, with skin and hair of a certain color, and with other special qualities which are hereditary.

Your first environment

When you started as a single cell, you immediately began to develop. For four months you were an embryo. At about the end of the fourth month your heart began to beat. Then, by definition, you became a fetus. You remained a fetus until the time of your birth, when you were known as a baby.

As an embryo and fetus you had a certain environment. Your environment was everything around you which affected you. Part of your environment was the material supplied by your mother's blood.

So your first environment gave you certain materials to work with. Your cells used these materials. You grew and developed within the pattern set by your genes.

Your supply of nutritional materials provided by your mother was part of your environment. If the supply was adequate, to that extent your environment was good. You were well supplied with material for your growth. If the supply was inadequate, your environment was bad to that extent. You were cheated out of nourishment you needed.

So, regardless of your genes, your first environment had much to say as to whether your cells were good or bad.

You and your environment at birth

When you were born you were a small but complex body known as a newborn baby. You had some built-in reactions such as coughing and sneezing. You reacted to certain changes in your environment and to changes inside you. You cried and you moved. You were quite helpless. Much care was required just to keep you alive.

What was your environment at birth? Part of it was the food, drink, and other materials you swallowed. Part of your environment was the air, gases, odors, dust, and other matter you breathed. Part was the sounds, words, music, and noises you heard. And everything you touched, or which touched, moved, or struck you, was part of your environment.

Your environment at birth was rather simple. You didn't need much more than to be warm, clean, comfortable, and filled with the proper food and drink. As long as you were supplied with these things, you were happy. Anything more, such as movies, fireworks, and gay parties would have been unnecessary or harmful.

What you were after birth

After your birth—say two years after—you were about 33½ inches tall and you weighed about 26 pounds. You walked and talked. You were not much more complex than at birth. But now your complex nature showed itself more clearly. Your reactions to your surroundings were more complicated.

Your environment, however, had changed. First, your surroundings supplied many things you didn't know about in the first few months after birth. Dogs, cats, and other children, for example. At the age of two, you could run around. You could get into new and different places. You could visit the neighbors' homes and the neighborhood stores.

Further, you operated on a higher level. You saw many new, odd, and strange sights. You touched and felt new and different things. Some of these you put in your mouth and swallowed. You breathed in new and different substances—dust, odors, and fumes. You heard strange sounds. You were struck, hit, cut, bumped, and rubbed by new and different objects.

What you are now

Now you are a skin-sack full of cells.

Of course, to be technical, we should realize that your skin is also made up of cells.

Possibly we should say, "Now you are a total of innumerable cells—skin cells, nerve cells, blood cells, muscle cells, bone cells, gland cells, mucous membrane cells and so on," naming all the groups of cells in the body.

You are bigger than you were when you were two years old, of course. Also your environment has become much more complex. But the most important thing is this: Now the responsibility for your health, growth, development, and behavior lies with you!

A famous experiment

Dr. Alexis Carrel, with the assistance of Charles Lindbergh, made a famous experiment. There is a very short account of the experiment in Dr. Carrel's book, *Man, the Unknown*.[1] You will be interested in this experiment because it has to do with cells. Also, because you are a skin-sack full of cells, it has to do with *you.*

In this experiment Dr. Carrel kept some cells of a chick embryo alive and multiplying in his laboratory for over 30 years! He proved that he could, if he wished, keep the cells alive indefinitely.

Suppose, now, that you were an assistant to Alexis Carrel. We shall say that you went to work near the end of the experiment.

Let's imagine that these were your instructions: Dr. Carrel said, "Observe this flask. It contains nutritive fluids and gases, called the 'medium.' Immersed in the medium is a fragment of heart from a chick embryo.

"Your job is (1) to protect the cells (fragment of heart) from physical damage, (2) to keep harmful materials away from the cells, (3) to remove waste products from the medium as fast as they are formed, and (4) to put into the medium everything the cells need for their life and growth.

"If you do your work well, and you maintain the cells in good condition, you will be well paid. You will also receive a special bonus. If you fail in any one of your four responsibilities you will be punished."

You take the job and accept the responsibility.

At the end of a week you make your first mistake. While

---

[1] (New York: Harper & Brothers, 1939), p. 173.

carrying the flask from one table to another, you trip. You bump the flask and injure the cells. You are punished.

Later on you became careless. You use the wrong water. This puts some harmful substances into the medium. The cells are damaged and you are punished.

All goes well for a while. Then you fail to remove the waste matter which has accumulated in the medium. The waste matter damages the cells. You are punished.

Finally comes your fourth error. You fail to put into the medium some of the nutritive substances needed by the cells. Again the cells are harmed and you are punished.

With your four mistakes, however, you learn to do your job well. You keep the cells in fine condition. You receive your special bonus.

You use your imagination

One day, while tending the cells, you get an idea. You think:

"This flask is a container. In the flask is the medium. Immersed in the medium are the cells. All I do is the four things I was hired to do. Apparently if I do that, the cells will live forever.

"There isn't much difference between me and this flask.

"The flask is made of glass. My outer covering, which represents the flask, is made of skin.

"Inside the flask is the medium. Inside my outer covering is *my* medium—my blood.

"The cells in the flask are surrounded by the medium. *My* cells are surrounded by my blood.

"The cells in the flask group together to make the fraction of chick embryo. In me my cells group together to make my bones, nerves, and various organs.

"In the flask the medium supplies the cells with their nourishment, and it removes the waste products as they are formed.

"In me my blood supplies my cells with their nourishment,

and it removes the waste products formed by the processes of living.

"What will happen (1) if I protect *my* cells from physical damage? (2) If I keep harmful materials out of *my* blood? (3) If I remove the waste materials from *my* blood as fast as they are formed? (4) If I supply *my* cells with everything they need for their growth and development? I should stay physiologically young, strong, and with an abundance of energy and good feeling as long as I live. But even more interesting— perhaps I would live forever!"

Then you think, "Wait a minute, now. 'Forever' is a long time. After all, I'm getting a late start. I'll settle for 100 years.

"Here's something else, too," you continue. "Caring for my own cells will be a different matter from taking care of the cells in this flask. For the care of the cells in the flask I have been told exactly what to do. But to care for my own cells I'll have to get all the information myself. I'll have to set up my own procedures. I'll have to determine exactly what to do. Then I'll have to get myself to do it. If I don't care for my cells properly I'll be punished. I'll get sick. I'll hurt. I might even die prematurely.

"But, on the other hand," you think, "if I care for my cells correctly, my rewards will be great. I should always be well and strong. I should have an abundance of energy. I should always feel good. I should be happier. I should live longer. I should get a lot more out of life."

Your procedure

"So," you say to yourself, "this is what I shall do: I shall learn exactly what I must do if I wish to take good care of my cells. At the same time I shall learn how I am to be punished if I fail to care for my cells properly. This is very important. It will warn me away from the things I should not do. It will make it easier for me to take proper care of my cells.

1. Facts About Your Cells And Their Physical Damage

In your imagination you worked in the laboratory with Dr. Carrel. There you were punished if you allowed the cells in the flask to be damaged physically.

Now you must protect *your* cells from physical damage.

Your cells are damaged physically when they are cut, bumped, frozen, scalded, burned, bruised, shocked with electricity, or burned with acid.

How You Are Punished If You Allow Your Cells To Be Damaged

Painful experience has already taught you the results of cell damage. You know how heat, acids, and sharp instruments can destroy your cells. You know how much it hurts.

You may not know, however, that your teeth can be damaged by acid.

Dr. Oliver E. Byrd, in his *Nutrition Sourcebook*,[2] page 155, makes this report: When sugar reaches the tooth surface an acid is produced which decalcifies the tooth substance. The result is tooth decay.

A study Dr. Byrd reports on page 157 shows that the sugar may be refined or unrefined (raw). Either one can bring about the tooth decay.

On page 161 Dr. Byrd reports a study by Carey D. Miller of the University of Hawaii. This study indicates that certain fruit juices, including orange juice, cause from three to seventeen times more erosion of tooth enamel than do equivalent amounts of the whole fruits.

Your punishment for the physical damage to your teeth is tooth decay.

Now think about other parts of yourself. Think about your arms, your legs, or your torso. You know from experience what can happen when you allow these parts of yourself to be dam-

---

[2] (Stanford University Press, 1955).

aged physically. Suppose the cells in your arms, legs, or torso
are bruised, cut, burned, or crushed. Then you are in pain. The
pain may be excruciating. You may be confined to bed. You
may have to go to the hospital. This is your punishment.

As the result of an accident you may lose part of yourself.
You may lose an arm, a leg, or an eye. Or you may be killed
outright. This, also, is your punishment if you allow your cells
to be damaged physically.

2. Harmful Materials And Your Cells

In the laboratory you were punished if you didn't keep harmful substances out of the medium and away from the cells. Now
you are punished if you don't keep harmful materials out of
your blood stream and away from *your* cells.

You Can Eat Or Drink The Harmful Materials

In order to stay alive, you have had to learn about many
harmful materials. With others you may not be so familiar.

You know, of course, about the out-and-out poisons. They're
marked with a skull and crossbones. You have been trained
to avoid them.

The harmful materials may come in water. If you drink
water which contains the harmful materials, you introduce
them into your blood stream.

The poisons may come on your food in the form of sprays
and insecticides. Farmers use poisonous sprays to kill the bugs
on their crops. If the food still carries the poisons when you
eat it, you may get some of the poisons into your blood.

The harmful material may come *in* your food. It may come
in the form of preservatives which make the food keep better,
and bleaches which make it look better.

If you eat food which contains harmful materials some of
the harmful material may get into your blood and damage your
cells.

Harmful Materials In Your Lungs

You can breathe harmful materials such as fumes, polluted

air, smoke of all kinds including tobacco smoke, and poisonous gases. This brings the harmful materials into contact with your cells.

Harmful Materials Through Your Skin

You can introduce harmful materials into your blood through cuts and openings in your outer covering.

You can cut or break your outer covering in many ways. Often you simply damage a lot of cells, which grow again. But in other cases harmful substances enter your blood through the opening. Germs may also be admitted in this manner.

How You Are Punished If You Allow Harmful Materials To Reach Your Cells

If you allow harmful and poisonous materials to enter your blood, they damage your cells.

As the result of the cell damage you may be in pain. You may be greatly weakened. You may experience a *slow* and painful, or a *quick* and painful, death.

If you allow your skin to be damaged so that harmful materials or germs enter your blood stream, your punishment may be a bad case of blood poisoning. If not cared for properly you may die.

If you breathe smog, fumes, and certain gases into your lungs, you may greatly damage your lung cells.

According to a study reported in the *Nutrition Sourcebook*, page 58, if you smoke excessively you will be punished in a variety of ways. It is reported that the excessive use of tobacco lowers the blood sugar level. For this reason, it is said, chain smokers frequently feel faint and giddy. Sometimes they may have cold sweats and attacks of dizziness. As a rule, it is reported, the chain smoker is irritable, shows evidence of high tension, and suffers from wear and tear on the heart muscle.

In addition, there is evidence that the combination of air pollution and heavy cigarette smoke may bring on chronic bronchitis.

Then the chronic bronchitis may turn into emphysema. The

person with emphysema gasps for breath. His actions are restricted because of his shortness of breath. If you have ever had your breathing obstructed, or if you have seen a person with a severe case of emphysema, you know how terrible it can be.[3]

Dr. E. Cuyler Hammond, in 1963, was the Director of Statistical Research of the American Cancer Society. At the 17th annual clinical meeting of the American Medical Association, he presented his report of a special study.

The study compared mortality rates of pairs of subjects—one a smoker and the other a non-smoker—matched for such characteristics as age, race, height, native or foreign born, residence (urban or rural), religion, education, marital status, alcohol consumption, sleep habits, exercise, nervous tension, drug use, sickness, and other factors.

The study involved 36,975 non-smokers and 36,975 men who smoked a pack of cigarettes or more per day.

During the course of the study, twice as many smokers died as did non-smokers.

Cause Of Death	Deaths Among Smokers	Deaths Among Non-Smokers
Lung cancer	110	12
Emphysema	15	1
Aortic aneurysm	30	8
Coronary artery disease	654	304
Other causes	576	329

Further, it was found that 50 percent more heavy cigarette smokers than non-smokers were hospitalized.

Above are some of the ways you may be punished if you allow harmful materials to reach your cells.

3. Waste Products In Your Blood

When, as we imagined, you worked in the laboratory, you were punished if you allowed too many waste products to ac-

---

[3] "Emphysema, Little Known Disease of the Lungs, More Deadly Than TB," by Nate Haseltine, *The Washington Post* (*L.A. Times*), June 9, 1963.

cumulate in the medium. You learned that the faster the waste products accumulate in the medium, and the more poisonous they are, the quicker they kill the cells.

Now *you* are punished if you allow the waste products to accumulate in *your* medium—in your blood.

Also, the more waste products you accumulate in your blood, and the more poisonous they are, the more you are punished.

How The Waste Products Are Produced

Waste products form as the result of the processes of living. How you live determines, in great part, the quantity of waste products.

How You Can Increase The Waste Materials In Your Blood

Here's an easy way to increase the amount of waste products inside you. First, weaken yourself in some way. For example, indulge in excesses of various kinds over a period of time. You might overwork, carouse too much, drink, or smoke too much. You might worry too much. Do anything which will bring about sufficient weakness. Then the lack of energy results in sluggish inner functioning. The sluggish functioning results in a deficiency of both secretions and excretions. With insufficient excretion the waste products pile up inside you.

Here's another easy way to increase the waste materials inside you. Simply eat too much. The overeating crowds your digestion. Then the undigested, uneliminated, and decomposing material accumulates.

How You Are Punished If You Allow The Waste Products To Accumulate

When enough of the decomposing material accumulates inside you, it produces toxemia.

Toxemia is a general intoxication due to the absorption of bacterial products (toxins). It is a form of blood poisoning in which the toxins produced by certain microorganisms enter the blood.

Toxemia is also defined as toxins in the blood stream. This includes uremia and any poison in addition to bacterial toxins.

Suppose you allow waste matter to accumulate inside you.

Then your blood stream carries the poisonous waste material to every part of you. All your parts, including those buried deepest (your brain, spinal cord, your heart, bones, joints and glands) are exposed to the attack of the poisons and the invading organisms.

What happens when the infectious material in your blood reaches an organ or a nerve, nerve sheath, muscle, lining, or gland which has been weakened in some way? What happens when these cells can't fight off the invading microorganisms? The microorganisms invade your bones and joints, brain and spinal cord, blood vessels and heart.

When this occurs you will be the unhappy possessor of some disease. What disease? It can be almost any disease you can think of. The disease you get depends (1) on the condition of your cells and your various organs and (2) on the disease-producing agent which happens to be active at the time.

But regardless of the disease, you are sure to suffer.

Note that Dr. Carrel mentioned the waste matter in connection with the cells in his laboratory. He said, "The rate of accumulation of the waste products in the medium, and the nature of these products, determine the characteristics of the duration of the tissues."

We can assume that the same holds true for *your* cells. Then the rate of accumulation of the waste products in *your* blood determines the length of life (the characteristics of the duration) of *your* cells.

Allow enough waste products to accumulate and you shorten the life of your cells. Or you kill them outright. And remember! When this happens *you suffer*. If the waste matter and the toxins kill enough of your cells, *you die*.

That is how you are punished if you allow the waste products inside you to accumulate.

4. The Starvation Of Your Cells

In our imagination you worked in the laboratory as an assistant of Dr. Carrel.

You were punished if you failed to supply the cells in the flask with all their nutritional needs.

Now you are punished if you starve your own cells. The more you starve your cells, the more severely are you punished.

How You Can Starve Your Cells

Look in any elementary book on nutrition. There you learn how you can starve your cells. Just don't give them enough protein, carbohydrates, fat, vitamins and minerals, oxygen and water.

a. The proteins

Proteins are highly complex substances. They are found in all living cells. They are the structural building blocks of the body. You need them to build and maintain your cells and tissues.

The proteins also help oxidize the carbohydrates and especially the fats in your diet.

Protein is important in your blood. Ninety-five percent of the hemoglobin molecule is protein.

Then there are the antibodies. When you have measles, the antibody for measles is formed. This is a specific substance which stays in the blood. Then you are not likely to have the disease again. In the same way, antibodies protect you from other diseases you have had in the past.

The antibodies in your blood stream are protein in nature.

The chief components of proteins are the amino acids.

Some 22 amino acids occur in nature. Eight amino acids have been found to be essential in human nutrition.

Certain amino acids may be lacking, or in short supply, in your diet.

How You Are Punished If You Don't Supply Your Cells With Enough Protein. Fail to supply your cells with enough protein and this is what happens: You may be punished with a case of edema—a swelling of the hands, face, and legs. Later on you might experience pallor, weakness, or anemia. If you are an older person you may experience retarded bone healing, poor wound healing, and decreased resistance to infections to a greater extent than in a younger person.

Dr. Munro, in his book, *Man Alive You're Half Dead!* [4] says the following conditions can result from a deficiency of protein: General debility, swollen ankles, high blood pressure and heavy, drooping eyelids (pages 51–56).

Dr. McCarrison, in his *Nutrition and Health,* [5] tells us that

> . . . the insufficient ingestion, absorption or assimilation of protein, or of proteins of the right kind, will tend to degradation of vital processes; a degradation manifested in stunting of growth, poor physique, lack of energy, resource and initiative, digestive disturbances and impaired action of glandular organs. To these there may be added a lower resistance to infection.

Suppose the protein deficiency is such as to interfere with the operation of the antibodies. The antibodies may not be able to protect you from the recurrence of a disease.

b. The carbohydrates

The carbohydrates are the "go" foods. Mainly they supply energy. The carbohydrates we use as food are the sugars and the starches.

How You are Punished If You Don't Ingest Enough Carbohydrate Food. The carbohydrate foods are cheap, plentiful, and popular. They make up about half of the usual American diet. It is not likely, therefore, that your supply of these foods will be deficient. If anything, it is probable that you will eat too much of these foods, or the wrong kinds.

However, if you should happen to get too little of this food

---

[4] (Bartholomew House, Inc., 1950).

[5] Sir Robert McCarrison and H. M. Sinclair, *Nutrition and Health* (Faber & Faber, 1953), p. 39.

you may experience what is known as "low blood sugar." You may feel unduly weak and fatigued.

c. The unsaturated fatty acids

There are two fats. One is *saturated*. Examples are suet and the hard fat of animal meats, coconut oil, and hydrogenated vegetable oils.

The other is *unsaturated*. "Unsaturated" means the absence of hydrogen at certain places in the long chain of carbon atoms. Examples of unsaturated fats are linseed and cottonseed oil, corn oil, and safflower oil. The fats in fish and seafood are predominantly unsaturated.

There are three unsaturated fats which play a role in your nutrition. You must have them in your diet for the nourishment of your cells. They have an essential place in the covering of your nerves. They assist greatly in burning the storage fat of the body.

How You Are Punished If You Fail To Supply Your Cells With Enough Of The Unsaturated Fatty Acids. Fail to get enough unsaturated fatty acids and you may be punished by contracting a skin trouble of some kind, possibly something akin to eczema.

d. The vitamins

The need in human nutrition has been established for the following vitamins: [6]

Vitamin A	Vitamin D	Vitamin B-1 (Thiamin)
Vitamin K	Vitamin B_6	Vitamin B_2 (Riboflavin)
Niacin	Vitamin C	Vitamin B_{12}
Pantothenic Acid	Vitamin E	Folic Acid

The need for the following is strongly suspected, but it has not yet been established:

Rutin	Inositol	Para-aminobenzoic Acid

---

[6] *Food. The Yearbook of Agriculture, 1959.* Department of Agriculture, Washington, D. C.

How You Are Punished If You Don't Supply Your Cells With Enough Vitamins, And In The Right Balance. VITAMIN A: If you don't give your cells enough vitamin A over a long enough period, you may be punished by having trouble with your windpipe or bronchial tubes. You may develop small abcesses in your tonsils. You may experience night blindness. You may develop a mild or severe eye infection. A severe infection may lead to total blindness. VITAMIN B1 (thiamin), VITAMIN B2 (riboflavin), and/or NIACIN: What happens if you give your cells less than the minimum daily requirement of B1, B2, and/or niacin over a prolonged period of time? As punishment you may experience one or more of these symptoms: Nervousness, loss of appetite, neuritis, loss of muscle tone, digestive upsets, diarrhea, vague aches and pains, fatigue, irritability, headache, dizziness, dryness of the hair or skin, mental depression, insomnia, indigestion, loss of weight, constipation, weakness, reddening of the lips or sores about the angles of the mouth, swelling and redness of the tongue, or inflamation of the mouth. VITAMIN C: What happens if you supply your cells with less than the minimum daily requirement of vitamin C over a long enough period of time? You may be punished with one or more of these conditions: Dental caries (bad teeth), anemia, defective teeth and gums, sponginess of the gums, soreness and bleeding of the gums, pyorrhea, some gum infections, loss of appetite, or local hemorrhages of the mucous membranes of the nose, mouth, gums, and about the face. VITAMIN D: As an adult, if you get enough sunshine on your skin, you should get sufficient vitamin D. If you give your cells less of this vitamin than they need you may be punished with a case of osteoporosis (abnormal porousness of bone). This is the cause of rickets in children. VITAMIN E: Give your cells too little vitamin E for too long a time and you may be punished by muscle weakness and degeneration. Also certain of your nerve centers may be affected.

If you are a woman you may not be able to carry a pregnancy through to a full term. If you are a man you may become sterile.

The Vitamins Work Together. We must not assume, from the above, that the vitamins work separately. The effects of vitamins overlap. In ordinary living no disease or ailment is caused entirely by the lack of any one vitamin.

e. The minerals

The need in human nutrition has been established for the following minerals:

Calcium	Phosphorus	Iodine
Copper	Iron	Potassium
Manganese	Zinc	Magnesium
Sodium		Cobalt

The need for the following minerals is suspected but not yet proved:

Nickel   Fluorine   Vanadium

How You Are Punished If You Fail To Supply Your Cells With Enough Of The Right Minerals. CALCIUM AND PHOSPHORUS: If you fail to supply your cells with enough calcium you may be punished by having your nerves become irritable. You may have some pains you would not have otherwise. Your heart may not function properly.

Calcium and phosphorus are both important for the growth and maintenance of the bones and teeth. If you fail to supply your cells with enough calcium and phosphorus, and in the right balance, you may have poor teeth. You may have poor or crooked bones. Also your blood may not coagulate properly. Your muscles may not function well. IRON: Fail to supply your cells with enough iron, over a long enough period, and you may be punished with iron deficiency anemia. Your blood may not be as good as it should be. IODINE: If you don't give your cells enough iodine your punishment may be a goiter. All your life processes will operate below par. You may have trouble with low-grade microorganisms (germs) and an unclean blood stream.

Here again we should note that many of the minerals work together. They also work, as a team, with the vitamins. Researchers find it difficult to determine the exact contribution of some of the minerals, and the punishments which come from a deficient supply of one individual mineral.

f. Oxygen

To care for your cells adequately, you must supply oxygen to every one of them. The oxygen is drawn into your lungs as you breathe. It goes through the walls of the air cells and is absorbed by your blood. Then the oxygen is carried to your cells by a compound composed partly of iron.

You know already how you are punished if you don't give your cells enough oxygen. You suffocate.

g. Water

About one half of the water in you is in your cells. The rest of it surrounds the cells or is in the blood vessels, in the plasma, and in certain cavities of your body.

Water is obviously a very important element both for your cells and for your total operation. If you don't give your cells enough water they begin to dry up. Give them *no* water and you die.

5. Failure To Eat The Right Food

When you fed the cells in the flask in the laboratory, your job was easy. You just poured in some established preparation.

If you didn't put the right preparations into the medium at the right time and in the right quantities, you failed as an assistant. You were punished.

Now, when you wish to feed your own cells, it isn't so easy. Now you don't have any established, simple formula you can eat or drink. You eat all sorts of food and you drink many different kinds of liquids.

Nevertheless, if you don't eat the food that gives your cells what they need, you are punished. If your failure is great, you are punished severely.

How You Can Eat The Wrong Foods

The wrong diet for you is food which does not supply your cells with all their nutritional needs.

One of the easiest things you can do is eat the wrong food. All you have to do is eat the standard American diet.

Go to any grocery or supermarket. Select foods you like, which you eat by habit, which look good, which are widely advertised, which are eaten by the people around you, which are cheap and which are sold in bright packages. Choose foods and soft drinks you find in any snack bar. Choose foods which are easy to chew, easy to prepare or already prepared. Choose carbohydrate foods which are soft and sweet. Select your food in this way and you will get some food which is right for you. But you will also get a lot of food which is wrong for you.

a. White flour foods are wrong for you

Consider the matter of processed food. For many years a tremendous argument has been raging.

It all started in the early days when the processors first removed certain parts of the grains when they made flour. They did it to make the flour look better and keep better.

Then a few crusaders took up the gauntlet. They investigated. They supplied the public with books and articles. These told the people that their bread and other processed foods had been robbed of vital elements. The books reported case after case where people became ill while eating quantities of the processed foods over an extended period. The crusaders proved their point.

Now the millers enrich their white flour. They put back into the refined flour certain items, and in certain quantities. Most of the white flour products you buy in the corner grocery have had some basic nutritional items returned to the flour.

Certain government and other authorities now say that our

present processed food is every bit as nutritious as natural foods.

On the other side, the advocates of natural food point out that if you take out several items from the whole grains and put back only some of them, you don't have what you started with. Something important is lost.

Along this line you should find some of the reports in Dr. Byrd's *Nutrition Sourcebook* of interest. Read them. On page 161, for example, Dr. Byrd reports the results of an interesting study. Laboratory animals were fed processed grain in the form of cornflakes, wheat flakes, and oatmeal. Other similar animals were fed the whole grain products. The animals fed the processed grains—the cornflakes, wheat flakes, and oatmeal—had about 50 percent more dental decay.

Would you like to know more about what can happen to your teeth and to your physical make-up when you eat the wrong foods? Then be sure to read *Nutrition and Physical Degeneration* [7] by Dr. Weston A. Price.

Dr. Price visited many different parts of the world. He studied different groups of native people, their native foods, and the physical condition of the natives who ate the foods. He also studied the physical condition of the natives after they had eaten the white man's food for a few years. What he found will amaze you. The book contains interesting facts and descriptions, together with 154 pictures. You will want to read the text. But even if you simply look at the pictures and read the captions you will get the message.

b. *Sugar and sugar foods are wrong for you*

What about candy, syrups, jams, jellies, icings, fillings, sweet rolls, desserts, pastries, soft drinks and so on, made with sugar?

Look into the matter yourself. See if you can find any nutritionist who advocates the use of sugar, either refined or in the natural state, to nourish your cells.

---

[7] (Published by the author, 1020 Campus Avenue, Redlands, Calif.).

Refined sugar foods don't nourish your cells. They give you energy. But while they give you the energy they may damage some of your cells. You can get just as much energy, without harm, as well as important food factors, from other foods.

c. Foods stored for long periods are wrong for you

There is no question about it. Certain food elements (largely vitamins) are lost by the lengthy storage of your food.

d. Foods grown on poor soil are wrong for you

It is fairly obvious that if the minerals aren't in the soil, they can't be in the plants which grow in the bad soil. If you eat a vegetable which is deficient in a mineral, you get less of the mineral than you should for your cells.

How You Are Punished If You Don't Eat The Right Foods

Imagine this situation: You eat the wrong foods all the time. You starve your cells. But in spite of that you live a long and healthy life. Finally, at the age of 110, you suddenly die easily and painlessly.

This would be much better than the present arrangement. But unfortunately this never happens. What really happens is quite different.

Suppose you eat the wrong foods. Suppose you don't supply your cells with their needed nutritional factors, and in the proper balance. Then different groups of cells (tissues and organs) give way at different times. You fall apart bit by bit.

At first, as you starve your cells, you don't know that anything bad is happening. You simply eat what you have always eaten and what the people around you eat. You may not know that you are depriving your cells of their nutritional needs. But your cells know. They begin to fail. The failure is slight, but it actually exists. It can be shown by the proper analysis of the cells.

Suppose you continue to starve your cells. You then bring about further changes—biochemical changes. Now your inner chemistry begins to fail. But you may still not know that anything bad is going on inside.

Imagine that you continue to starve your cells for their needed nourishment. Now you begin to see some evidence of your cell starvation. You find yourself with one or more of the troubles listed in Section 4 of this chapter, under the heading "Starvation Of Your Cells." You will note that some of the troubles listed, such as neuritis, headaches, constipation, digestive upsets, mental depression, dizziness, and anemia are reasonably serious. They may be painful. They hold you back and make it harder to get the most out of life.

Now you can feel and see the bad results of your cell starvation. Do you immediately change your eating habits and begin to nourish your cells? We hope so. But you may not. You may still not know that you are bringing the troubles upon yourself by starving your cells.

As you continue to starve your cells, month after month and year after year, you may experience other troubles. You may find yourself with pyorrhea, chronic throat trouble, or night blindness. You may develop high or low blood pressure, heart disease, a stomach ulcer, arthritis, or cancer. Or you may develop an anatomical lesion. This is a gap in the tissue. Examples of an anatomical lesion are leukemia, falling hair, cataract, brittle bones, and loss of hearing or eyesight.

Is there no escape from these punishments other than to supply your cells with all their nutritional needs? In some cases there is a partial remedy. Sometimes, as various groups of cells deteriorate or become diseased, you can have a surgeon cut them out. This may prevent your immediate death. You may then limp along in a weakened condition for a long time. But you will still suffer. You will get far less than you should from life.

The Development Of A Germ Disease

To make matters worse, as you drop down from the normal condition of perfect cells through the various stages of cell starvation and depletion, you invite infections. You lay yourself open more and more to the possibility of invasion by germs.

It's Like A Battle

It's as though you are in a battle with a vicious enemy. You are protected by an army of your soldiers. The soldiers are equipped with hand grenades, pistols, rifles, and machine guns.

Supply your soldiers with the weapons and ammunition they need. Then they keep off the enemy and you are safe.

Fail to supply your soldiers with their needs and the enemy enters their ranks. If the enemy can overcome enough of your soldiers the whole battle is lost.

In the same way, fail to supply your cells with all their needs and your cells can't protect you from the invading infections.

When the germs take over, everyone, including the doctor, gives his attention to the germ disease. Everyone tends to forget that it was the worsened condition of the cells, due to lack of needed nourishment, that made the invasion of the germs possible.

How You Are Punished By Infections

What specific troubles can you have as the result of infections?

Fail to nourish your cells properly over a period of years and you may experience a disease of the upper respiratory tract—colds, flu, grippe, pneumonia.

How Do You React?

Do you think, "This is terrible! Why don't the doctors do something about all this? Why don't they find something for me to take? They should give me some scientific elixir which will keep my cells normal no matter what I do. Then I could eat, drink, and smoke as I wish and as much as I wish. I could overwork, overplay, undersleep, and overworry. But I'd always be well."

Here are the facts: Many new medical discoveries will be made. But no such magic elixir will be found. Nor will medical science change the basic operation of the human body.

There will always be one, and just one, basic procedure for the preservation of your good health and the avoidance of physical trouble. You must take care of your cells!

Does this depress you? Do the facts given in this chapter make you feel that all is lost?

Do these facts convince you that if you neglect your cells as does the average person, you are sure to get yourself into some kind of physical trouble?

If your answer is "Yes" you are right!

Neglect your cells as do most people, and you are sure to pay the price, just as they do. You will become ill. You may die prematurely.

But there's no reason to become depressed. All is *not* lost! You don't *have* to neglect your cells. As we shall see, you can learn to lead a busy life and still take good care of your cells.

6. Too Much Stress

You have often heard someone mention "stress" and the "stress of life." Now you need to know the relationship between stress and your cells.

A new concept of stress appeared about 1950 as a milestone in medical research.

Dr. Hans Selye, internationally famous endocrinologist of the Institute of Experimental Medicine at the University of Montreal, gives his definition of stress. In his book, *The Stress of Life*,[8] he defines stress as a "rate." It is "essentially the rate of all the wear and tear caused by life." It is the rate of the wear and tear experienced by your cells.

Situation 1

Suppose you live the most serene life you can imagine. You have no troubles or problems. You are protected from the weather and shielded from all annoyances.

Even with such tranquility, some of your cells wear out or break down as you go about your daily living. Because of your sheltered life, however, and the absence of severe stress-producing situations, your wear and tear is slow.

---

[8] (New York: McGraw-Hill Book Company, Inc., 1956).

Situation 2

Now we shall say that you live a very active life, possibly in a large city.

First, you work hard. You move around. You do things physically. As a result, you experience a certain rate of physical wear and tear—a certain stress.

Second, you are in a variety of situations which increase the rate of your physical wear and tear. These are the situations which "take something out of you."

Stress-producing situations are of two kinds—emotional and physical.

Most of the situations disturb you emotionally. Here are some examples: You experience stress when, as a parent, you have an ill child. When, as a golfer, you are off your game. When you have a marriage problem. When you have job trouble. When you drive in heavy traffic.

Then there are the times when you are bothered by a dripping faucet, by a quarrelsome drunk, or by a prying neighbor. Also the times when you are insulted, or when you are exposed to noise and overcrowding. In all these situations your cells are subjected to greater wear and tear.

Here are some situations which can produce extreme emotions, and consequently more stress. They greatly increase your rate of physical wear and tear: You are about to lose your business. As a father you see your child drown. Your fortune is wiped out on the stock exchange. You borrow $100,000 and you can't pay it back. You are on the verge of divorce. You have a delinquent child held by the authorities.

You always experience greater stress (a more rapid physical wear and tear) when you are nervous, jittery, frustrated, ill, excited, worried, anxious, fearful, or in pain. And strange as it may seem, you also experience increased physical wear and tear when you are joyful and pleasantly excited.

Here are some of the situations which affect you physically. These greatly increase your physical wear and tear: When you

experience winter cold or summer heat. When you have your
teeth extracted. When you are ill with a serious germ disease.
When you undergo an operation.

In Situation 2 you experience stress—a rate of physical wear
and tear—which can be very great.

How You Are Punished If You Experience Too Much Stress

If the stress is severe enough and it lasts long enough, you
may experience one of what Dr. Selye calls the "diseases of
adaptation." These come as the result of your inability to adjust
yourself to the stress. Among these diseases of adaptation Dr.
Selye lists many nervous and emotional disorders, high blood
pressure, gastric and duodenal ulcers, and certain types of
rheumatic, allergic, cardiovascular, and renal disease.

Now turn back to the troubles listed in Section 4, "The Starvation of Your Cells," and in Section 5, "Failure to Eat the
Right Food." Those troubles can all come from a deficiency of
essential food factors. There you will find listed, among others:
nervousness, high and low blood pressure, stomach ulcers,
arthritis, and heart disease.

Almost *any* disease can come as a result of the accumulation
of waste products in the blood. The illnesses which develop,
then, can include: nervousness and emotional upsets, high and
low blood pressure, ulcers, rheumatism and arthritis, the aller-
gies, and diseases of the heart.

Now compare all three lists.

From all this we see that you can mistreat your cells in
three different ways and get very much the same result.

THREE WAYS YOU CAN BRING ILLNESS UPON YOUR-
SELF. First, you can make yourself ill by starving your cells.

Second, you can bring sickness upon yourself by allowing too
much wear and tear on your cells.

Third, you can bring upon yourself a variety of physical
troubles by killing your cells with excess waste products.

In the first case, you fail to build your cells *up*.

In the second case you tear your cells *down*.

In the third case you knock your cells *out*.

THE MOST POPULAR WAY TO BECOME ILL. Note that the causes of illness all work together.

(1) Many people starve their cells for important nutritional substances.

(2) At the same time, these people are in situations which bring about considerable stress.

(3) These people also allow too many waste products and toxins to accumulate in their blood stream.

In addition and at the same time,

(4) Many of these people hurt their cells by indulging in certain harmful habits and by permitting accidents to occur.

(5) Many of them damage certain cells and organs by taking into themselves harmful materials of various kinds.

The result? Millions of people have some physical trouble.

You know this is true. Just think of the millions of people in hospitals, in sanitariums, in rest homes, and ill at home. Think of the people who are treated by doctors and dentists. Think of the millions of people to whom our medical commercials are directed. Think of your friends and relatives who are ill. All these people have less power to get the most out of life.

YOU CAN CHOOSE YOUR ILLNESS. Suppose you are subject to the five causes of illness mentioned above. Suppose you are subject to them daily for a period of years. What will happen? You will make yourself ill. But not only that. You may be able to predict your ailment!

Suppose you elect to have a case of scurvy. That's easy. Along with subjecting yourself to the other four causes of illness, simply deny your cells their minimum supply of vitamin C.

Would you prefer heart trouble? That should be easy too. Subject yourself to the five causes of illness for a long time. Overexpose yourself to them. Put on fifty or seventy-five pounds of excess weight. Then go out and run a mile!

On the other hand, you might not get exactly what you asked for. You might try for lung cancer and get emphysema instead.

You might try for arthritis and get neuritis. If you tried for a stroke you might get heart trouble, or vice versa.

But of this you can be certain: Subject yourself to all of the five causes of physical illness at once. Do this over a period of years. Then you will certainly wreck one of your organs, or you will bring some disease upon yourself. You will greatly decrease your power to get what you want out of life.

HOW YOU ARE REWARDED IF YOU TAKE GOOD CARE OF YOUR CELLS. The earlier you start (and the earlier your parents started), and the better you care for your cells, the greater will be your rewards.

Take good care of your cells and you can make better and wiser decisions. You will find it easier to start good new habits and to stop bad habits. With good sound cells you will find it much easier to handle people and to deal with them effectively. You will be able to study and remember better. You can render more service. You can do more work and earn more money. You can handle your money more wisely. You will have more power to get what you want out of life. Life will be more interesting.

Further, when you take excellent care of your cells, over a long enough period, you are rewarded with good feelings. You really enjoy life. You have a good appetite. You have plenty of strength and energy. You enjoy your work more. Little things don't bother you so much. You get along better with people. You have a much better chance for success and happiness and to get what you want from life.

The secret of the proper care of your cells

The purpose of this chapter and the next one is to show you how to increase your ability to get the most out of life.

In this connection you should know about a man in Los Angeles. This man, almost up to the time he was 70, had instructed the Los Angeles police force in judo. Some time after he was 70 years old he was still big, strong, full of energy, and hard as iron. When asked how he did it he would reply, "Just remember it isn't a pill. It's a program."

The secret of taking proper care of your cells, the secret of keeping yourself out of all physical trouble, and the secret of more power to get what you want out of life is the same. It isn't any one particular activity. It's a *system!*

You have two choices

In this chapter you learned the important facts in the general field of physical fitness. Now you have two choices. You can decide to take good care of your cells and keep yourself out of physical trouble. Or you can decide to continue with your present habits. You can decide to follow a *system* which will keep you well and strong and out of physical trouble. Or you can continue with your present way of life.

The suggestion

Hold your decision. Don't try to decide now.

Instead, read the next chapter. There you will see the proposed plan for the proper care of your cells.

Chapter 7

TURN ON YOUR PHYSICAL POWER

*In this chapter you learn the Five-Step
Plan to develop more physical power.
You also learn how to keep yourself out
of physical trouble.*

There was once an institution for the feeble-minded.

When an inmate was ready for parole, this test was used:
The prospective parolee was led to a large iron bathtub. He
was told to turn on the water and fill the tub. If he first put
in the plug, and then turned on the water, he was paroled. If
he turned on the water without putting in the plug, he stayed
in the institution.

How to get more power

You want to fill yourself with physical power. You need this
abundance of physical power to help you get the good things of
life.

You add to your physical power by doing certain things and
by meeting certain requirements.

You drain off your power by allowing physical troubles to
continue or to develop.

What will be your approach? Will you first put in the plug?
Will you eliminate your present physical troubles while you
develop more power?

Or will you let physical troubles drain off your power as fast as you develop it?

Suppose you now have some physical ailment. What should you do? Put yourself in the hands of a good doctor and do as he says. The doctor is the expert. Let him take the responsibility for getting you over your trouble.

While the doctor treats you, is there anything *you* should do? There certainly is. You should keep yourself out of all *future* physical trouble.

It's silly to pay a doctor to get you over one physical trouble while you develop more physical troubles for the doctor to cure!

Suppose you aren't ill. Suppose you enjoy what everyone calls "good health." Must you do anything then? Certainly. Develop *more physical power*. At the same time keep yourself out of all physical trouble.

Study the plan

In the last chapter you learned the important facts in the general field of physical fitness. Now you must learn all about the suggested plan. Then make your wise decision.

THE FIVE-STEP PLAN TO INCREASE YOUR PHYSICAL POWER
TO GET THE MOST OUT OF LIFE

A. *Protect Your Cells From Physical Damage*

Train yourself to live without bumping, bruising, cutting, burning, scalding, pinching, crushing, breaking, abrading, scraping, or in any way damaging your cells.

Learn to avoid all accidents.

If you drive a car, avoid automobile accidents. Learn to drive so your car never so much as touches another car.

Wear shoes which keep your feet comfortable and free from all damage to the cells of your feet.

Avoid anything which, when put into your mouth, damages your teeth.

Start right now and see how long you can go without harming your cells. Can you go for two full weeks?

If you can't live for at least two weeks without in some way hurting your cells physically, turn back to Chapter 4. Use enough of the Procedures. Train yourself to avoid physical damage to your cells.

B. *Keep Poisons And Harmful Materials Out Of Yourself And Away From Your Cells*

Be like a food inspector. Study the food you eat for evidence of contamination and harmful materials. Scrutinize everything you eat. Keep harmful materials of all kinds out of the food you send down to feed your cells.

Avoid foods which contain preservatives, bleaches, and other materials that could poison your cells. Avoid vegetables with traces of insecticides remaining on them.

Even if a certain food contains only a small amount of harmful material, when you eat many such items the harmful materials add up.

Also be like a public health inspector. Watch for impure water, spoiled food, or food containing germs that could harm your cells. Avoid them.

Avoid tobacco and tobacco smoke. In volume 22 of *Federation Proceedings*,[1] under the heading "Catecholamine Excretion in Smokers and Nonsmokers," Dr. T. C. Westfall and D. T. Watts report on some scientific experiments.

One experiment showed that the inhaled smoke of one cigarette will increase the epinephrine (adrenaline) content of the blood many times. Epinephrine is a body-regulating chemical. It is a powerful stimulator. Very small amounts are essential. But the constant presence of larger amounts is harmful.

Also avoid all types of foul air as much as you possibly can. One of the harmful substances here seems to be acrolein, found in smog, automobile exhausts, and in industrially polluted air.

---

[1] Federation of American Societies for Experimental Biology, "Catecholamine Excretion in Smokers and Nonsmokers," *Federation Proceedings*, XXII, 509.

C. Keep The Waste Materials Inside You To A Minimum And Remove Them As They Form

1. Keep all harmful waste products to a minimum.

Three Priceless Rules: (1) Before you eat a meal, ask yourself this question, "Have I felt really good since my last meal?" If your answer is "No," don't eat. Don't take any food drink either. Just wait until the next meal time.

(2) Before you eat a meal, ask yourself, "Do I have a really good appetite?" If your answer is "No," don't eat. Wait until the next meal.

(3) Near the end of every meal, ask yourself, "Am I satisfied without being really full?" If your answer is "Yes," stop eating.

Follow these rules and you will do much to avoid the accumulation of waste products.

2. Relax.

When you are tense, your muscles develop waste material, just as they do in any muscular activity. The more tense you are, the more waste material you produce. All this waste material is then ready to interfere with the normal life and growth of your cells.

Conversely, the more relaxed you are as you go about your living, the less waste material you generate to harm your cells.

Stay relaxed.

3. Sleep well.

Sleeping is something like eating. You can eat a lot of food and not get the basic nutritional substances you need. You can also have a lot of the average sort of sleep and not get enough real rest and rejuvenation.

There is bad sleep just as there is bad food. But there is this difference: You can look over a list of available foods and select the best. But you can't select bits of good sleep from a night full of bad sleep!

Good sleep is the only kind you want.

Dr. Selye suggests that you watch your critical stress level, just as a wise person watches his critical quota of cocktails. Avoid undue stress and you won't get so keyed up. If you don't get keyed up, you sleep better.

Dr. Edmund Jacobson, in his book *You Must Relax*,[2] tells exactly how to relax for better sleep.

4. *Exercise.*

You are descended from a long line of ancestors reaching back for thousands of years. Your "way back" ancestors lived a life of almost constant movement. Most of this was outdoors. Almost always it involved the use of their large skeletal muscles.

They hunted wild animals, swam streams, climbed trees, threw rocks, fought, built rough shelters, prepared food, walked, ran, and carried heavy loads for long distances.

You are the product of millions of years of natural selection. This natural selection was directed toward a certain end. For the most part, it was directed toward the production of people equipped for strenuous exercise and heavy physical work. Consequently, you were not designed to sit at a desk and read or write. You are designed to use your big muscles, and to use them strenuously.

True enough, through neglect, you may have allowed your muscles to weaken. But the fact remains that you come from a long line of ancestors whose muscles were designed for strenuous physical movement.

So be sure to get plenty of physical exercise. You need it partly to keep your muscles strong, partly to maintain good blood circulation, partly to promote normal elimination, and partly to develop the energy you need to get the most out of life.

There are many types of exercise from which you can choose.

2 (New York: McGraw-Hill Book Company, Inc., 1957).

According to your age, physical condition, environment, and physical needs you can walk, hike, swim, or play an athletic game such as golf or tennis. You can ride horseback, do exercises with weights and other equipment in a gymnasium, ride a bicycle, walk up and down stairs, or do yoga exercises.

Many people like the yoga exercises because they emphasize deep breathing (to give you more oxygen), elimination, and relaxation. Further, you can do the yoga exercises wherever you are. You can do them in the middle or at the end of a busy day, for relief from tension. All you need is a space on the floor and a mat. You can make the exercises very mild or quite strenuous. You can enjoy them at any age.

If you would like to try the yoga exercises, get a copy of Indra Devi's book, *Yoga for Americans*.[3] This book gives a six-week course in the yoga exercises. From the book you can learn the exercises, one step at a time, in your own home.

To learn more about other types of exercise, consult the reference librarian in your local public library.

No matter what type of exercise you choose, remember this: Start easy. Almost always, when a person starts a new type of exercise, he experiences some muscular soreness. But don't let the soreness stop you. Persist through the soreness.

If it is indicated, have a doctor supervise your exercise at first.

5. *Posture.*

In addition to your exercise, be sure to maintain a good posture. To develop power, this is as important as physical exercise. As a matter of fact, when you always hold yourself in the proper sitting, standing, and walking posture you get a lot of physical exercise. In this connection be sure to read *Exercise Without Exercises*,[4] by S. Arthur Devan.

---

[3] (Englewood Cliffs, N. J.: Prentice-Hall, Inc., 1959).
[4] (Dodd, Mead & Co., 1944).

6. *Elimination.*

It goes without saying that your elimination should be adequate. It should be a natural process. Keep it normal without the use of laxatives or other unnatural aids.

Notice also that constipation is listed in the previous chapter as one of the indicators of nutriment deficiency. This means that your full nutrition is important for your proper elimination.

7. *Deep breathing.*

In grammar school you learned about the importance of fresh air. Your blood must be supplied with an abundance of oxygen. It is important for the life and operation of your cells. You must have it for power and energy.

In addition, certain waste materials are eliminated through your lungs.

You may find it helpful to take an occasional big breath of fresh air. Even an occasional good breath of fresh air is a help.

Breathe deeply and get plenty of fresh air into your lungs.

8. *Drink enough water.*

You also understand the importance of sufficient water. You need an adequate supply for the elimination of waste materials and for your cells.

D. *Supply Your Cells With Everything They Need For Their Complete Nourishment*

   Eat the right foods for you

To be sure you eat the right foods, proceed as follows:

1. Make a list of *all* the different foods you actually eat now in the course of a week.

2. *Remove* certain items from your list. You must remove these foods for two reasons. First, they don't give your cells maximum nourishment. Second, you must make room in your stomach for the foods that do nourish your cells.

It's like taking counterfeit money out of your pocketbook. You take the counterfeit money out partly because it's worthless, and partly so you can fill your purse with good money.

Remove from your food list:

(a) White sugar and the "foods" which contain sugar, such as candy,[5] ice cream, sherbet, jelly, jam, soft drinks and some alcoholic drinks, cake icing, and pastries.

(b) Corn syrup and other sugar syrups.

(c) White flour, together with the "foods" made from it, even if the flour is "enriched." These foods include white bread, rolls, buns, biscuits, crackers, macaroni, spaghetti, hot cakes, pastry of all kinds, pie, and cake. Also Mexican, Italian, and other food made from refined flour.

(d) White rice.

(e) Remove all artificial "foods" designed to replace natural foods.

When you remove these items, does it seem to leave nothing on your list? Do you have visions of starving to death? If so, be of good cheer! In a moment we shall refill your list.

If you would like to be sure that you remove from *your* food list *only* those items that should be removed and *all* the foods you should omit, consult a well-trained nutritionist.

Do you find it difficult to remove certain items? This exercise may help you:

Look at each of the foods on the list below. Ask yourself this question: "Do I eat this food?" If your answer is "Yes," ask yourself "Do I eat this because it nourishes my cells?" If your answer is "Yes," put "NC" after the item.

If your answer is "Because it tastes good," "Because I always have," "Because it's served everywhere I go," "Because it's cheap," or "Because it's easy to prepare," put an "O" after the item.

---

[5] *Time*, April 26, 1963, p. 85, reporting on the consumption of candy in Britain, said the English, in the previous year, ate an average of 8 ounces of candy weekly, nearly double the consumption of any other European country and well above the 5.6 ounces a week for the United States. The dentists blame candy for the fact that Britain leads the world in bad teeth.

Here are the foods:

White bread	Cookies	Fresh fruit
Buttermilk	Jelly	Maraschino cherries
Milk	Brown rice	Syrup
Pickles	Cooked vegetables	Sugar
Doughnuts	Cake	Whole wheat bread
Pancakes	Pie	Yogurt
Maple syrup	Butter	French pastry
Potatoes	Lasagna	Honey
Baking powder	Raw vegetable	Waffles
biscuits	salads	Coffee
Meat	White rice	Jello
Rolls (white	Tea	Raw nuts
flour)	Ice cream	Chicken
Preserves	Eggs	Jam
Sherbet	Wheat germ	Salted nuts
Spaghetti	Soft drinks	Fish
Candy	Canned foods	Gelatin
Puddings	Macaroni	Dried fruit

Be sure to follow this suggestion. You can mark the list in a few minutes.

You should look on every item marked with an "O" with grave suspicion.

3. *Add* to your food list all the foods not on it, which you *should* eat to supply your cells with adequate nourishment.

How can you learn what foods to add?

Study books written by the experts. They list the basic foods the average person should eat in order to feed his cells properly. You can find many of these books in your local library.

In these books you will find a list of the foods everyone should include in his diet.

These are some of the foods you should *add* to your food list if they are not on it: Milk, eggs, butter, and cheese; fresh or raw fruits and vegetables; fresh meats and sea foods; and whole wheat bread and other whole grain products made from fresh, ground flour.

Be sure to consider the advisability of adding honey and the sweet fruits to your diet in place of sugar.

But remember this: "One man's food is another man's poison." Milk, for instance. Also, you should not be satisfied with just the foods recommended for the average person. You want the foods which will be best for *you* and *your* cells. For this you should consult an expert nutritionist. This is someone professionally engaged in investigating and solving problems of nutrition. Such an expert can tell you the *specific* foods *you* should add to your diet.

Can you secure the right foods?

Now comes an important question. Is it *possible* to obtain the right foods for the nourishment of your cells? Fortunately, in the United States at least, it *is* possible.

In this country our supply of food is like our supply of books.

Every year, thousands of bad books are printed. But in spite of this, you can still find plenty of good books to read. All day long, and every day, you can read excellent literature which is also varied and interesting.

In the same way, every day our grocery shelves are loaded with a lot of bad foods. But in spite of this you can still find plenty of good food to eat. You have only to pick and choose. Every day you can eat three meals of delicious food, with plenty of variety and the nutritional factors your cells must have.

That's the nice thing about living in a free country. Just as you can choose your own reading material, you can also choose your own food.

The disadvantage is this: If you read the wrong books or eat the wrong foods and you get yourself into trouble, you have nobody to blame but yourself.

You can't blame the publishers if they print and distribute

trashy and demoralizing books. They are in business to make
money, not to supervise your reading.

Neither can you blame the food producers and processors if
they provide certain foods which supply but little nourishment
for your cells. They are in business to make money, not to
nourish your cells.

In the same way, since this is a free country, you can't expect
the Federal government nor your local government to supervise your diet. Those who are responsible for your government
would *like* to have you eat the right food. This would nourish
your cells and make you a better citizen. But you can't expect
your government to *force* you to eat the right food. That isn't
their job.

The Federal government and the local authorities see to it
that plenty of food is available to you. It's up to you to select
your food wisely. It's up to you to nourish your cells.

4. Eat the foods on your completed food list and, as far as
possible, no other foods.

a. When you are at home: Develop the habit of eating only
the foods on your final list. Chapters 4 and 5 will help you
develop the habit.

b. When you eat out and you can select your food: Eat
where you can get the food items on your list. You may have
to take food from home if you can't get the right food in any
other way.

c. When you eat out and you don't have complete control
(as when you are a guest): (1) If you are in a restaurant, follow your food list as best you can without making yourself too
conspicuous. (2) If you are dining in someone's home, do the
best you can without offending your hostess.

d. Think of what you eat in terms of bites of food. You can
hold only so many bites. Each mouthful of food, therefore,
must nourish your cells.

e. When you start to eat something, think, "Does this bite

of food contribute its share of nourishing substances to my cells?" If the answer is "No," drop that item. Select a food item that does give your cells the nourishment they need.

Chew your food

We shall now assume that you have plenty of good food, properly prepared, and ready for your use. Now you must eat it.

It isn't enough just to swallow the materials your cells need. When you swallow your food your inner organs must be able to make the food elements available to your cells.

Suppose you put each bite of your food into an insoluble capsule. Then you swallow capsule after capsule until you have swallowed a complete meal. When you do this, have you nourished your cells? Of course not. Nothing can get out of the capsule.

In the same way, if you swallow each mouthful of food whole, can your inner organs prepare it properly for your cells? Possibly, if it is all meat. But not if you eat a well-balanced meal. Then you have to chew it well. First, you must chew it to let the starches start their digestion in your mouth. Second, you must chew it enough to make it easy for the inner organs to do their work. They must extract the nutritional materials your cells must have and pass it on to them.

Now you should know about Fletcher.

Horace Fletcher was born in 1849. He was an enthusiastic traveler. He circled the globe four times and penetrated into obscure parts of Mexico, Central America, Japan, and the Dutch Indies. With headquarters in San Francisco he made a fortune manufacturing printer's ink. He was one of the founders of the famous Bohemian Club of San Francisco. He was an athlete, art correspondent, and painter.

In 1895, at the age of 46, he was turned down by a life insurance company because of overweight, poor digestion, and frequent illnesses.

He tried several cures, without success.

Then he investigated the problem of human nutrition. He

was interested mainly in the part the mouth and teeth play in the work of digestion. Apparently he reasoned that the better your digestion, the better your cells are nourished.

He paid special attention to the slow and thorough chewing of food. His habit was to chew each mouthful of food thoroughly (40 times, as a rule). He removed from each mouthful of food, before he swallowed it, anything (such as vegetable fibers) which could not be liquefied.

His physical condition improved. Apparently he helped things along with physical exercise. He celebrated his 50th birthday by riding two hundred miles on a bicycle.

Then he spent most of his time telling people about his ideas. Soon "Fletcherism" and "Fletcherize your food" were common expressions.

He published five rules: (1) Eat only when genuinely hungry. (2) Eat whatever appeals to your appetite. (Concerning this rule, remember that the food available in 1895 was quite different from our present supply.) (3) Chew your food until it swallows itself. (4) Eat only when free from anxiety, depression, or other preoccupation. (5) Eat to enjoy food.[6]

Learn from Fletcher. Follow his five rules. But what about rule No. 2? If you eat to please your appetite, won't you fill up on candy, doughnuts, mince pie, and cookies? Here's the answer: Adjust your diet. Supply your cells with all their needs. As you do this, more and more the foods that appeal to your appetite are the foods that nourish your cells, and vice versa.

Also note rule No. 5. If you eat to enjoy your food, you won't give a bite of food two chews and then swallow it. You get no enjoyment that way. Instead, you will follow Fletcher's rule. You will eat to enjoy food. Then you will really taste and enjoy every bite. You will enjoy each bite until it is completely liquefied.

---

[6] Based on the biography of Horace Fletcher in *Dictionary of American Biography*, ed. Allen Johnson and Dumas Malone (New York: Charles Scribner's Sons, 1931), VI, 464–65.

Separate the high starches and the high proteins

Here's another way you can help your food nourish your cells. This, too, will give you more power.

Dr. Daniel C. Munro, in his book *Man Alive You're Half Dead* (get the revised edition), has much to say about diet. He suggests that high starches (breads, potatoes, cereals, sweets) should not be eaten at the same meal with high proteins (meat, eggs, fish, cheese). The rule is based on the fact that the proteins are digested largely in the stomach. Carbohydrate foods are digested largely in the small intestine. If you eat them together, the carbohydrates, while passing through the stomach, interfere with the digestion of the proteins.

Dr. Munro mentions other combinations which should be avoided—pure fats (butter, cream, bacon fat) with high starches (potatoes, bread, cereal, sweets).

He also recommends the separation of acids and carbohydrates. When you eat buttermilk, orange juice, lemon juice, grapefruit, or vinegar, he says, eat no high starches at the same meal.

These may appear to be nonsensical recommendations. But the place to test these rules is with a person who has a weak digestive system.

To the person with a strong stomach these rules may seem like a lot of foolishness.

Does this separation of the high proteins and the high starches seem like a lot of nonsense to you? If so, read Chapter 7 of *Man Alive You're Half Dead*. Then check the facts with a good nutritionist. Experiment for yourself. Finally, make your decision. Decide whether you will, or you will not, do your best to separate the high proteins from the high starches and not eat them at the same meal.

Don't overeat

Dr. Josef Brozek is reported by Dr. Byrd, in his *Nutrition Sourcebook*, page 223, as saying that the dietary intake should be reduced by about 7½ percent for each decade after 25. By the age of 70 a person should eat only about 70 percent of what he ate at 25.

Eat simply

Dr. George Gallup made a study of oldsters. He used his famous sampling technique. He studied men and women 95 years of age and older. He reports his findings in his book *The Secrets of Long Life.*[7]

Are you interested in remaining physiologically young and vigorous while you live to a ripe old age? If so, be sure to read this book.

Dr. Gallup studied the diet of the oldsters. He reports that the really meaningful finding is this: The old people insisted on "plain" food. Apparently they didn't care much for crepes suzette or other fancy cooking.

You can learn from these people who lived to be at least 95.

If you wish to nourish your cells, eat plain food. It will give you more power to get the most out of life.

Add the supplements you need

Suppose, now, that you have eliminated all the wrong foods from your diet. Also, let's assume that you have added all the good foods *you* should eat.

You follow the Three Priceless Rules.

You chew every mouthful of food thoroughly.

You make a real effort to separate the high proteins from the high starches at each meal.

You don't overeat and you eat simple foods.

If you have done all this, does it guarantee that *your* cells will receive all the important nutritional substances they need?

Not necessarily. Other factors may prevent it. For one thing, you may need more of one or two dietary elements than the average person. Then you can eat an average amount of the right foods and still not get enough of all the necessary food elements for *your* cells.

---

[7] Dr. George Gallup and Evan Hill, *The Secrets of Long Life* (Bernard Geis Associates, 1960), p. 79.

You may eat the right foods but they may be wrongly prepared—possibly overcooked.

You may eat the right foods, but not in the proper balance. You may eat too little of certain foods and therefore get too small a supply of certain nutritional factors.

Some of the food you think is good may have been stored for a long time.

Without your knowing it, some of your food you think is as nature made it may have been processed in some way.

Some of your food may have been grown on poor soil.

So you may make a real effort to supply yourself with a diet which contains everything your cells need. Through no fault of yours you may fall short of your goal.

If you own an automobile, you know your car is supposed to run well on a good grade of oil and the right gasoline. Sometimes, however, a car develops sticky valves or noisy lifters. Then the attendant at your service station suggests the addition of certain special oils and other preparations to give your engine what it needs. These you buy in addition to your regular oil and gas. You give them to your engine as "extras."

In the same way, many people, for one reason or another, add certain vitamin, mineral, amino acid, or unsaturated fatty acid supplements to their regular diet.

Some people add the basic nutritional element to their diet just to be sure they are on the safe side.

Other people add the nutritional elements because they have been advised to do so by their physician or nutritionist.

Some people are under special stress. To compensate for the extra wear and tear on their cells and because they can't eat any more food, these people supplement their diet with certain concentrated nutritional preparations.

Many people add the nutritional elements in concentrated form because they have evidence that their cells are not receiving an adequate supply. For example, they may experience some of the indicators of vitamin-mineral deficiency listed in Chapter 6.

Should *you* supplement your diet? Should you add the basic nutritional substances in concentrated form? To get the answer you can follow either or both of two procedures.

First, you can consult a good nutritionist, have a thorough examination, and let the nutritionist advise you.

Second, you can investigate the matter yourself. You can learn the nutritional elements which may be in short supply in your diet. Then you can add them as supplements.

The best procedure is this: First consult a good nutritionist and follow his advice.

Then look into the matter yourself. Get all the facts. Check them with the nutritionist. Make some experiments yourself under his direction. Learn what supplements you should add to *your* diet.

But however you do it, supply all your cells with everything they need. Make all your cells strong and sound. Then keep them that way. Do this to avoid physical trouble and to develop your maximum power.

E. *Keep Your Stress To A Minimum*

It is foolish to build *up* your cells with good procedures and then tear them *down* with too much stress. You must, therefore, hold your stress—this "wear and tear"—to an absolute minimum.

(1) As much as you can, avoid all situations which bring about greatly increased stress. Examples are medical operations, extreme exposure to heat or cold, and situations which bring great excitement and deep anxiety. (2) Avoid stress situations by making wise decisions. (3) Minimize the effect of the stress situations you can't avoid. Do this by keeping your cells in tiptop condition as explained in this chapter. Do it by supplying your cells with extra materials for their use in times of stress. Do it by the use of extra hormones if prescribed by a physician. (4) Stay relaxed. Watch yourself for evidences of tension. Be on the lookout for nervous movements, whistling and humming, muscles held tense, toes held up from the floor, and for feet or hands in constant motion. Watch for squints

and frowns, teeth grinding together, loud talking, and exuberant actions. When you notice any of these signs of tension in yourself—relax! Keep yourself relaxed at all times. (5) Think positively.

This you must *not* do: Don't rely on sedatives or tranquilizers to ease the tension. Learn to live correctly.

We have now considered the five steps of the proposed plan to provide you with excellent cells, to keep you out of physical trouble and to give you the power to get the most out of life.

Will you follow this plan?

Before you make your decision, here is—

A Final Reminder

If you neglect your cells you must accept the consequences. Your punishments come in the form of pain, illness, disability, weakness, and a shorter active life. You may find yourself in a wheel chair or in a hospital bed. You may have a physical or mental breakdown. You may wake up in an institution for the insane. You may come under the surgeon's knife. You may die.

On the other hand, *take good care of your cells and your cells will take care of you!* They will give you more power to get the most out of life.

NOW DECIDE!

A plan has just been proposed. It is proposed that you:

A. PROTECT YOUR CELLS FROM PHYSICAL DAMAGE

B. KEEP POISONS AND HARMFUL MATERIALS OUT OF YOURSELF AND AWAY FROM YOUR CELLS

C. KEEP THE WASTE MATERIALS INSIDE YOU TO A MINIMUM AND REMOVE THEM AS FAST AS THEY FORM

D. SUPPLY YOUR CELLS WITH EVERYTHING THEY NEED FOR THEIR COMPLETE NOURISHMENT

E. KEEP YOUR STRESS TO A MINIMUM

Use the 18 Steps of the Decision-Making Technique (Chapter 2) and make your wise decision.

STEP 1. Get all the important facts about the situation which suggested the plan.

(a) You may not, right now, make as many wise decisions as you should.

(b) Your present physical condition may not be as good as it should be. You may even be ill.

(c) You may not feel as good as you should.

(d) You may make too many mistakes.

(e) You may not have enough energy.

(f) You may not be getting the most out of life.

Determine the facts about *your* situation.

STEP 2. Gather the important facts about the proposed plan.

You know all about the plan. It is described in full above.

STEP 3. Determine the goal of the plan.

The goal of the plan is the excellent care of your cells. Indirectly, the goal is to keep you out of physical trouble. Primarily the goal is to give you the extra physical power you need to get the most out of life.

STEP 4. Check the goal of the proposed plan with your personal goals.

If your goal is to be well and strong, this plan harmonizes with it. If your goal is to get rid of some ailment, the plan harmonizes. If your goal is to get the most out of life, this plan is for you.

But suppose your goal is to maintain whatever health you can and your present energy, using nothing but your present procedures plus a doctor and medicine when you get sick. Then the plan doesn't fit your personal goal.

STEP 5. Be sure you have enough general knowledge in the field of the plan.

In Chapter 6 you reviewed some important facts in the general field of physical fitness. Now the question is: Do you have *enough* facts to enable you to judge this plan?

You must answer that question yourself. If you think you have enough facts, you have only to continue with the 18 Steps and make your decision. If you think you need more facts in this field, get them now.

Suppose you encounter some nutritional statements or medical opinions which seem to contradict the facts given in Chapter 6? If you do, consult a well-trained nutritionist. Get the facts!

STEP 6. Be sure your physical condition and qualifications are right for the plan.

It doesn't take much physical energy or special physical qualifications to follow this proposed plan. Unless you are almost dead, your physical condition and your physical qualifications should be right for this plan.

STEP 7. Be sure you have enough control of the plan.

If you should accept this plan, would you have sufficient control?

Are you now restricted in your movements? Are you so restricted that you cannot protect yourself from physical damage? Must you swallow everything given to you, so you can't keep harmful materials out of your blood stream? Must you breathe whatever fumes or smoke come your way? Can you do nothing to promote the proper removal of the waste materials as they accumulate in your blood? Must you eat only the food provided and add no food supplement? Can you do little to control your stress? If so, you will not have sufficient control to enable you to use the plan.

But if you live under normal conditions you will have more than enough control. All you have to do is get your back up and put the plan into effect.

STEP 8. Be sure you have the right thinking habits to enable you to carry out the proposed plan successfully.

The important thing here is your habitual mental attitude toward the improvement of your physical condition and the development of physical power.

Suppose you always think, "Why should I worry about my

health? If I get sick I'll take some medicine or lay off work for a week. If I get too bad, I'll call a doctor."

If that is your habitual way of thinking this proposed plan doesn't fit this thinking habit.

If, however, you habitually think, "I want to improve my health and physical condition and to have more energy," your thinking habit is right for the plan.

STEP 9. *Be sure your emotional habits are right to enable you to carry out the plan.*

It's hard to see how your emotional habits can be wrong for this plan. But even should they be wrong, you can balance this off with the realization that if you follow the plan your emotional reactions should improve.

STEP 10. *Be sure your physical habits are right for the plan.*

If your present habit is to conform to custom and to eat what is put before you, your physical habit is not right for the proposed plan. Neither is your habit right if your usual procedure is to sit as much as possible and to exercise as little as you can.

If your physical habits don't happen to be right for this plan, remember that you can change your habits. You should find it easy to establish the new habits you need. Use the methods suggested in Chapters 4 and 5.

STEP 11. *Your environment must be right for the plan.*

Do you live in a home with a wonderful cook who prepares fancy dishes and who urges you to eat everything in sight? If so, your environment isn't right for the proposed plan. Neither is your environment right if you live in a boarding house or a retirement home, where set meals are provided.

However, if you live with people who are understanding and sympathetic your environment may be right for the proposed plan. This is also true if you live any place where you can choose your own food, exercise, and your other health needs. It's a help, also, if you have enough money to care for yourself properly. But even if you don't happen to have much money, you can still use most of the plan. You will be delighted when you realize how much of the plan you can use even on a small income.

STEP 12. Consider the possible rewards if the plan is successful.

You may have some trouble with this step.

Suppose that, all your life, you have neglected your cells. You have been up and around most of the time. You have gone to work nearly every day. But actually you have been only half well.

Now you are asked to imagine what it would be like to have all your cells in excellent condition. How can you imagine how it feels to have cells in excellent condition when you have never had them? How can you imagine the physical thrill which comes when you are really well and strong, with every muscle and organ perfect, if you have never experienced this condition?

Anyway, do your best. Try to imagine what it would be like to enjoy all the rewards which are yours when you follow the five steps of the suggested plan.

The possible rewards are excellent cells and all that goes with them—a good physical condition, freedom from health troubles, plenty of energy, better and wiser decisions, good feelings, and the possibility of remaining physiologically young while you live to a ripe old age.

As you consider the possibility of extending your life by the use of the Five-Step Plan, think of this: Dr. Edward Bortz, a past president of the American Medical Association and the American Geriatrics Society, said, "We are going to have to overhaul some of our supposedly sophisticated views of modern living.

"That more people don't reach the century mark," Dr. Bortz' report said, "seems to stem from the fact they are not willing to follow a regimen of proper diet, exercise, rest and recreation, coupled with the exclusion of stimulants, depressants and other excesses." [8]

STEP 13. Consider the penalties if the plan fails.

What are the penalties if the plan fails? None, really.

If the plan fails you might lose a little time, a little effort, and perhaps a small amount of money. Actually you have everything to gain and little to lose when you follow the plan.

STEP 14. Determine the odds in favor of the success or failure of the plan.

What are the odds in favor of the success of this proposed plan? Remember, the plan is a success if it enables you to take excellent care of your cells and to develop more power to get the most out of life. Nothing more is required to make the plan successful.

Now—what are the odds that, if you follow the proposed plan faithfully, you will take excellent care of your cells? Are the odds 100 to 1 for your success? Are the odds 1,000 to 1?

STEP 15. Figure out what the other fellow will do if you carry out the plan.

This is what he'll do: He'll kid you!

Just wear shoes that protect the cells of your feet from physical damage. If the shoes are unlike the prevailing style, the "other fellow" will ask you why you wear such "ugly" shoes.

Fortunately you can get shoes that fit your feet and which still conform reasonably well to the styles. To accomplish this, some people have their shoes custom made.

If you learn to drive a car well and you drive so as to avoid accidents, some people will criticize you. Those who want a thrill will tell you that you are overcautious or afraid to take a chance.

If you refuse sugar and sugar products, the "other fellow" will wonder why you are so "different."

If you refuse to smoke, some people may call you a sissy.

---

[8] *Los Angeles Times,* May 26, 1963.

Suppose you refuse to eat certain foods because you think they may contain harmful materials. Or you refuse to eat foods made from processed flour. The "other fellow" will call you a "food nut," a faddist, or a health crank. Some of your hostesses will say, "I just never know what to prepare for you. I haven't any idea what you will eat." Your friends will say, "Why can't you be normal and eat like the rest of us?"

Perhaps, in order to protect yourself from excessive stress, you refuse to carry on certain activities. The "other fellow" may make fun of you or call you a quitter.

If you take a nap in your office after lunch, the "other fellow" may kid you about loafing on the job.

If you decide in favor of the plan, get set for some good-natured, or not so good-natured, ribbing.

On the other hand, if you decide for the plan you will find plenty of people who will say you are smart. They'll give you a friendly pat on the back. They will admire you for your good sense.

STEP 16. *See how many other plans you can find which will take you to the same goal.*

Try to find other plans which will enable you to take excellent care of your cells and to develop more physical power. Find as many plans as you can.

STEP 17. *Use this same procedure (Steps 1 to 15) with each of the other plans. Find the best plan.*

See if you can find another plan which will give you excellent cells and more physical power, quicker and easier, than the plan offered here.

STEP 18. *Go off by yourself and make your wise decision.*

Follow the instructions in Chapter 2 and the suggestions in Chapter 3 for the correct use of Step 18. Be sure to use the 18 Steps. Don't let your habits decide for you! Remember that you can change your habits.

Use the Decision-Making Technique and make your own decision!

What to do if you decided against the plan

Did you decide against the plan? Did you decide that you would *not* follow the Five-Step Plan, take excellent care of your cells, and develop more physical power? If you did, this simply means that as of now, with things as they are at this time, you decided against the plan. Later on, when conditions are different, you may wish to change your decision. You may wish to make a real effort to keep yourself out of physical trouble and to develop an abundance of physical power. Should that time come, return to Chapter 6 and to this chapter. You can use the Decision-Making Technique again and make another decision.

In the meantime, if you decided against this plan, go right on to Chapter 8.

What to do if you decided in favor of the plan

Did you decide to accept the plan and to make a sincere effort to take excellent care of your cells? If you did, try these suggestions:

a. When you look at someone, don't think, "I wonder how healthy he is." Think, "I wonder how good his cells are." Observe the person carefully. See if you can determine the condition of his cells.

When you see a person eating, look at his food. See if you can tell how much of his food, and what part of his food, will nourish his cells.

When you see an older person, don't think, "I wonder how old he is." Think, "What is the condition of his cells?" Look for the signs which show that he is taking good care of his cells.

When you think of yourself don't ask, "How healthy am I?" Ask yourself, "What is the condition of my cells?" Watch for signs of cell weakness and cell strength.

When you have a physical examination, don't be satisfied

with a statement from the doctor such as, "You have such and such," "Everything is within normal limits," or "Considering your age, you're in good condition." Tell the doctor you want to know the condition of your cells—good, bad, or indifferent. *Note:* It is not easy for the doctor to give you this information. But he should be able to study you as a whole and make some shrewd guesses as to the state of your cells.

b. Go back to Chapter 4. Use the Keys given there and develop the *habit* of living by this Five-Step Plan for the development of excellent cells. Do it one step at a time. Take just one single act, such as taking some appropriate exercise every day, and make it a habit. Then take another—perhaps it's taking a nap after lunch, or rejecting sugar desserts. Make *it* a habit. Continue until you have all the individual habits necessary to make the use of the whole Five-Step Plan just one big habit.

c. Every day, read some of this chapter and Chapter 6. Let these chapters act as signals to help you follow the plan.

d. To help you follow the Five-Step Plan, be sure to read Chapter 15 of Dr. Gallup's *The Secrets of Long Life.* He tells about "The Conspiracy Against a Healthful Diet," "The Conspiracy Against Exercise," and "The Conspiracy Against a Calm Temperament."

e. See page 70 of the *Autobiography of Benjamin Franklin.*[9] There Franklin tells how he switched back and forth from the common diet to his special diets. It may help you.

f. Take it easy. Remember that Rome wasn't built in a day. Don't jump into the plan all at once. Ease yourself in a little at a time. Don't overdo any part of the plan. Be especially careful about this while you are getting started. Go at it gradually.

The important thing is to get started. Then add a little more

[9] (Garden City Publishing Company, Inc., 1916).

of the plan every day and every week. The more you do in this easy, gentle way, the more you benefit.

Every setting sun should find you farther along in the use of the plan.

What Will You Do With Your Extra Energy?

What happens when you improve the condition of your cells? You develop more energy.

How will you use this extra energy?

Use it to get more of the good things of life.

The suggestion

Now turn to Chapter 8. Learn how you can use your spare time to improve your cells, your habits, and your decisions.

Chapter 8

LET TIME BRING YOU WHAT YOU WANT

In this chapter you learn the six parts of the Time Plan. You learn how to make time bring you (1) more power, and (2) the good things you want from life.

You started your life with five obligations.

Your first obligation was to take excellent care of your cells.

When you met the requirements of this obligation you enjoyed the pleasures and satisfactions of good health. When you failed to meet your obligation you experienced pain and discomfort.

Your second obligation was to establish good habits.

When you built good habits you were rewarded in many ways. When bad habits appeared you were punished, either directly or indirectly.

Your third obligation was to make only wise decisions.

It didn't take you long to learn the advantage of wise decisions over bad decisions.

To this point we have discussed the first three of your obligations. Now we must consider your fourth obligation.

As usual we start with the proposal. In this case the proposal and your fourth obligation are the same—use your time wisely.

Your correct reaction to this proposal is to ask, "What is the proposed *plan?*" Then you must get the facts in the general field. Next learn all about the plan. Finally, use the Decision-Making Technique and make your wise decision.

Some facts in the general field

Here are some of the facts in the general field of time. To these add all the other facts you have now. Add all the facts you gather from other sources. You will then have enough facts to enable you to judge the plan wisely.

First Fact

You have 24 hours of time, every day, just as does everyone else.

Second Fact

Nobody seems to know just what time is.

Addison called time an "immense ocean." Theophrastus called it "the most valuable thing that a man could spend." Emerson called time something "which dissipates to shining ether the solid angularities of facts." Anatole France said time was "like a precious tissue which we embroider as we best know how." Franklin said that time is the "stuff life is made of." Sir James Jeans said that time was such a puzzle that "it brings our thoughts to a standstill." Ben Johnson called time "that old bald cheater." Keats called time "that aged nurse (which) rocked me to patience." Marcus Aurelius called it "a sort of river of passing events." Plutarch called time "the wisest counselor of all." Pythagoras called time "the soul of this world."

Third Fact

Although nobody knows what time really is, everyone agrees that "time waits for no man."

Fourth Fact

Time, in and of inself, has no value. You can't eat it, drink it, sell it, or trade it for something else.

Fifth Fact

Time is a period in which you have an opportunity.

When you awaken in the morning there lies before you, for 24 hours, a series of opportunities.

As you go through your day, for example, you have:

1. An opportunity to improve your cells through exercise.

2. An opportunity to strengthen a good habit or to weaken a bad habit.

3. An opportunity to nourish your cells—breakfast.

4. An opportunity to serve or to produce—your job or your vocation.

5. Several opportunities to make wise decisions.

6. Another opportunity to nourish your cells—lunch.

7. Another opportunity to serve or to produce—your job or your vocation.

8. Another opportunity to improve your cells through exercise.

9. Another opportunity to improve a good habit or to weaken a bad habit.

10. An opportunity to nourish your cells—dinner.

11. An opportunity to build a good habit, to acquire knowledge, to make a wise decision.

12. An opportunity to restore your cells through rest, relaxation, and entertainment.

13. An opportunity to restore your cells through sound sleep.

Sixth Fact

You have opportunities for service and production. These are your working time activities.

Seventh Fact

You have opportunities to restore your cells through rest and relaxation. These are your leisure time activities.

In your leisure time you are not obliged to do anything. You can loaf, rest, sleep, amuse yourself, and visit with your friends.

Eighth Fact

You have opportunities to improve yourself through study and practice. These are your spare time activities.

In your spare time you can learn to make better and wiser decisions. You can improve your habits. You can carry on activities which improve your cells. You can acquire knowledge.

Ninth Fact

Each opportunity can be assigned a period of time.

To your opportunity to improve your cells through exercise, for example, you may assign 15 minutes. To your opportunity to improve a habit you might allow 10 minutes. To the opportunity to nourish your cells (breakfast) you might set aside 30 minutes. For your first opportunity to serve or produce you may assign four hours.

In the same way you can allow a certain amount of time for each opportunity listed under the *Fifth Fact* heading above.

Tenth Fact

You can list your opportunities for each day in advance. When you assign a certain amount of time to each opportunity, you have an opportunity schedule.

Eleventh Fact

"Time is money," said Benjamin Franklin.

This is true because you can use your time to make money.

Suppose you waste your time. Then you lose the money you could have earned in the time you wasted. Or you miss the training you could have gotten in the time wasted. This training could have enabled you to earn more money.

Twelfth Fact

All your time is now filled.

Every moment of the day you are doing something.

You may be busy working, resting, loafing, watching TV, listening to the radio, reading whodunits, chatting with the neighbors, playing bridge, admiring the view from your front window, or daydreaming.

You are like a 24 hour radio station. The radio station has a program of some kind scheduled for every minute of the 24 hours. If the program manager wishes to add a new program, he must drop one already scheduled.

You, too, are doing something every moment of the day. If

you wish to make room for a worthwhile opportunity, you must give up a less desirable activity.

Thirteenth Fact

Time is eternal. Time stays.

We are ephemeral. We go.

Do you want something from life? You must get it now, while you are here.

Now you have some of the important facts in the general field of time. Be sure to add your own facts.

Next you must:

Prepare for the use of the plan

First you must know how much time, each day, you can allot to the pursuit of spare time opportunities.

To accomplish this, proceed as follows:

(1) Determine the amount of leisure time you have on each day of the week from Sunday through Saturday. Add the seven figures and you have your total leisure time for the week.

Let's say that on Sunday you *must* carry on certain activities. These fill 14 hours of your time. Subtract this figure from 24, the hours in the day, and you have 10 hours of leisure time on Sunday. This is time in which you can do as you wish.

We shall say that you have 5 hours of leisure time on Monday, 4 on Tuesday, 6 on Wednesday, 5 on Thursday, 6 on Friday, and 8 on Saturday. The total for the week is 44. You have, in this example, 44 hours of leisure time each week.

(2) Determine the number of hours of rest, play, and amusement you think you *must* have, each day of the week. Add the totals for each day and you have the total for the week.

On Sunday, perhaps, you think you *must* have 8 hours for rest, play, and amusement. On Monday you must have 3. On Tuesday you need 2. You need 5 on Wednesday, 3 on Thursday, 4 on Friday, and 5 on Saturday. The total for the week is 30 hours. In this example you think you must have 30 hours of rest, play, and amusement every week.

(3) Subtract the total hours found in (2) from the total found in (1). Now you have the number of hours of *spare* time you have available each week.

Your spare time, in this example, is 14 hours.

Assignment: Determine the actual amount of leisure time *you* have each week. This will be (1). Then determine the hours per week which you think you *must* devote to rest, play, and amusement. This will be your figure for (2). Subtract (2) from (1). This gives you the number of hours of spare time you have each week.

Next, you need to schedule your spare-time opportunities for the development of the power you need to get the most out of life. This is your opportunity schedule for the use of your spare time. As an example, it might look like this:

Sample Opportunity Schedule For The Development Of Power

Mon.	7–9 p.m.	Opportunity to improve ability to make wise decisions.
Tues.	6–7 p.m.	Opportunity to develop a new habit.
Wed.	7–9 p.m.	Opportunity to improve decisions.
Thur.	6–7 a.m.	Opportunity to improve cells.
Fri.	6–7 a.m.	Opportunity to eliminate an old, bad habit.
Sat.	10–12 a.m.	Opportunity to improve cells.

Note. When you think about some time you have available as spare time, don't think, "I have a free period from 7 to 8 this evening." Think, "From 7 to 8 this evening *I have an opportunity* to ———."

Don't think, "I must work for four hours this morning." Think, "This morning, for four hours, *I have apportunity* to serve or to produce."

Don't think, "For two hours this evening I should study."

Think, "This evening *I have a two hour opportunity* to improve myself."

Assignment: Make your own Opportunity Schedule for the Development of Power.

First determine how much spare time you have, each day, and when you have it.

Then, after each spare-time period, write the power-developing activity you select, as shown in the sample.

When you finish your schedule it should look something like the sample above. It will show when you have *your* spare time and the opportunities you have selected for the development of *your* power to get the most out of life.

The next step is to learn all about the plan:

The Four-Step Plan For The Right Use Of Your Time

A. *In Your Working Time Take The Best Advantage Of All Opportunities For Service And Production*

This is another way of saying, "Use your working time wisely."

Learn to render the best service.

If you aren't sure you know the field in which you can provide the best service, have a good vocational guidance examination with expert interpretation.

If you produce goods, develop the ability to produce the most and the best of your chosen product. Be sure it can be sold at a fair price and at a reasonable profit.

B. *In Your Leisure Time Find Your Best Opportunities For The Reduction Of Your Stress And The Restoration Of Your Cells*

This is another way of saying, "Use your leisure time wisely."

Learn to select the leisure time opportunities which will, at the same time, reduce your stress, restore your cells, and give you rest and recreation.

As an example, let's say that you are a dentist, a clerk in a store, or a letter carrier.

You want a leisure time opportunity which is good for you.

If you enjoy the activity you might read, collect stamps or coins, play bridge, watch television, or visit with other people. These all permit you to sit down. Each gives you a rest and a change.

C. *In Your Spare Time Use Your Best Opportunities To Develop More Power To Get The Most Out Of Life*

In other words, "Use your spare time wisely."

To use your spare time wisely, you have only to take advantage of the opportunities you listed in your Opportunity Schedule For The Development Of Power. Just follow your schedule. To make it easy to do this, use as many of the Keys from Chapter 4 as you need.

As you continue to follow your schedule, change to different opportunities as you need them to develop the most power.

D. *When You Have Enough Power, Use Your Spare Time To Get What You Want From Life*

Consult your list of personal goals. You made this list for Chapter 3.

Remove from your list any goal which you have reached or which no longer seems important.

Add to your list every other good thing you want. Now you have your list of the good things you still want from life.

Next, select the most important item on your list.

Determine what you must do to get the item. Schedule these activities in your spare time. Get this one item you want.

Then, in the same way, get everything else you want from life, one item at a time.

A possible book synopsis

What happens when a person uses the Time Plan? It might be like this:

Tom was 15 years old. When he returned from his mother's funeral he found $1.75 in the otherwise empty sugar bowl. He glanced at the picture of his father, who had died the year before. He closed the door of the single room with its dilapidated furniture and left the slums of New York forever.

Tom walked. He walked for days. He walked until he could walk no more.

Tom was sound asleep in the farmer's hay mow when the farmer woke him, pitchfork in hand.

The farmer took pity on Tom and gave him a job as a hired hand. He taught Tom to farm.

Tom looked upon this as a golden opportunity to learn a vocation.

In his leisure time, Tom occasionally played a game of checkers with the farmer.

But Tom used most of his leisure time as spare time. The farmer's wife was glad to teach Tom what she had learned in high school. Tom was a willing pupil.

Tom also used his spare time to study farm journals. He learned from them and from the farmer how to operate a farm.

Tom saved his money, bought two calves, leased some land from the farmer, and started his dairy herd.

Now Tom has the best dairy herd in the district and the best dairy business.

If you are a man between 65 and 80 years old, this may carry you back to your childhood. You will feel yourself sprawled on the floor reading the latest book by the noted minister and author. This man, whose life ended in 1899, wrote some 100 books which sold by the hundreds of thousands. You remember his name, of course. You will imagine yourself reading a book by Horatio Alger! All his plots were substantially the same—poor boy gets job, uses time wisely, comes out on top.

After you had read ten or fifteen of Alger's books you may have become bored by his banal, unsophisticated, platitudinous plots.

But as you think about it now, you realize something very important. Study person after person who uses the Time Plan and you are impressed by the similarity of results. People who use the Time Plan get what they want out of life with monotonous regularity!

Make your wise decision

Another plan has now been suggested. It is suggested that *you* use the Time Plan.

As in all cases when a plan is suggested for you to follow, you must not make a snap decision. Use the Decision-Making Technique and make a wise decision.

You can decide against the plan and forget the whole thing.

You can decide in favor of the plan and follow it.

But you need to make a clear-cut decision. You must not dillydally. You must not think, "Well, it does look like a good idea, but I don't know. . . . I guess I'll just wait a while."

Make a firm and wise decision, one way or the other.

You know the 18 Steps of the Decision-Making Technique by heart. If nothing else, you can look upon this as an excellent opportunity to practice the use of the Technique. The more practice you get, the better the decisions you can make.

So get the Four parts of the Time Plan firmly in your thinking. Then put this book down, use the 18 Steps, and make your wise decision.

The suggestion

Continue with your use of the Time Plan until you have the power you need to get the most out of life.

Then use the Time Plan and get more of the good things of life.

If one of the good things you want is money, or something which money can help you get, be sure to read the next chapter.

Chapter 9

MONEY—YOUR FAITHFUL SLAVE

*In this chapter you learn how to get
plenty of money and how to handle your
money wisely.*

Imagine this situation: You have a sudden and very urgent
need for $5,000 in cash.

Now consider the possibilities.

1) You have the money in your bank account. You have only
to cash a check.

2) You have ample collateral. You can borrow the money
and have the cash.

3) You have an idea which should produce a fortune. You
may be able to borrow the $5,000 from people who have faith
in you and in your idea.

4) You can borrow the money without security. You may
borrow it from someone who has faith in you and in your
willingness and ability to pay it back.

5) Someone, perhaps a relative, is willing to give you the
money.

The point is this: There are only two ways you can be *sure*
to have a certain amount of cash available for a sudden need
or opportunity. One is to have the money in the bank. The
other is to have ample collateral on which you can borrow
the cash.

Are diamonds a girl's best friend?

Diamonds, jewelry of all kinds, stocks, bonds, houses, factories, and office buildings are good. Any one of these could be a girl's good friend. But many people think there is just one *best* friend of a girl or of anyone else. Money!

Everyone doesn't agree, of course.

Some people quote the Bible and say, "the love of money is the root of all evil."

Along this same line, Sherwood Anderson said, "Money—the desire for money—the need of money has always been hurtful to me and to all men and women I have known."

On the other hand, many famous people seem to have been impressed with the virtue of money.

Byron said, "Ready money is Aladdin's lamp."

Said Emerson, "Money, which represents the prose of life, and which is hardly spoken of in parlors without an apology, is, in its effects and laws, as beautiful as roses."

Jack London is responsible for this: "It's money I want, or rather the things money will buy, and I can never possibly have too much. As to living on practically nothing, I propose to do as little of that as I possibly can."

Even Ovid, who lived almost 2000 years ago, had this thought about money: "How little you know about the age you live in if you fancy that honey is sweeter than cash in hand."

Which is better, much money or no money?

You can think of many people who have been ruined by money. You also know of people who have been ruined by the lack of money. Which is better, much money or no money? Fortunately, you don't have to decide now. Wait until you learn about the three Money Plans. Then use the Decision-Making Technique, and, for each plan, make your wise decision.

In Chapter 3 you were advised to make a list of your personal goals. You should still have this list. It is your own individual list. It is different from everyone else's.

We can, nevertheless, be reasonably sure of one thing. Your list almost surely contains one certain item—money.

You may want more money, or plenty of money, or millions of dollars. You may want to be able to take better care of your money. You may want to get out of debt. You may want financial security.

On the other hand, suppose there is no money goal on your list. Maybe there should be.

It is almost impossible, these days, to live without money. You need money to help you get many of the good things of life. You need money to keep some of the bad things out of your life. You need money to help others.

As was mentioned in the previous chapter, you started your life with five obligations. The first four were (1) to take excellent care of your cells, (2) to build good habits and to eliminate bad habits, (3) to make only wise decisions, and (4) to use your time wisely.

The proposal

It is now proposed that you live up to your fifth obligation. Your fifth obligation is to handle your money wisely.

To enable you to do this, and assuming that you could use more money, it is now proposed that you *increase* your income.

How do you react to this proposal?

It would seem that everyone should be most eager to increase his income. But this is not always the case. Many people have tried and failed. They are suspicious of any plan to bring in more money.

Other people have learned from experience that they must do something to get the additional money.

Since you have read this book to this point we can be sure of this: *You* react to the proposal by saying, "Before I make any decision at all, I must have the necessary facts in the general field of the plan. I must know all about the proposed plan. Then I can use the Decision-Making Technique and make a wise decision."

Some money facts

Here are some money facts to start you off. To these facts be sure to add all your own facts and all the facts you gather from other sources.

1. Your money consists of your currency (paper money and coins) plus what the banks or other institutions show in your checking or savings accounts.

2. Money is evidence of a debt. The debt is owed by people as a group (the community or society). It is owed to an individual person or group of people, for services rendered or goods delivered.

Let us say, for example, that you work for someone for eight hours.

You have now given your employer something he wanted and could use—your services. In exchange you want something *you* can use. But the man you work for (to whom you gave your services) doesn't have any service or commodity you want. So he gives you money. You take the money to someone else and exchange it for services or products you *do* want.

While you have the money it is evidence of a debt owed to you by the community. As soon as you give the money to someone and receive goods or services in place of it, the debt is paid.

3. As an employee you increase your income when you supply the community, as represented by your employer, with more and better services.

As an independent worker you also increase your income when you supply the community with more and better services. Or you supply more and better products at a fair price, and with a profit to yourself.

In return for your more and better services or your better

products, the community returns more money to you. You give more and you get more. That's the way you increase your income.

4. Money is time.

This is true because you can spend some money and buy time. As an example, suppose your situation requires the mowing of your lawn. If you do it yourself, it will require an hour of your time. If you pay someone else to do it, you have the time for another use. You have, in effect, bought an hour of time. Money is time.

You are now ready to learn The First Money Plan.

If you develop your income by investing or speculating, you will be more interested in the Second Money Plan and the Third Money Plan.

It is now assumed that you earn your income through your personal efforts, and that you need, or can use, more money.

With this plan and with the help of this book, your efforts to increase your income should be highly successful.

THE FIRST MONEY PLAN—*Increase your income*

Five separate steps make up this First Money Plan.

1. Make Only Wise Decisions. (Chapters 2 to 3.)

Learn to make only wise decisions in connection with your vocation. Wise decisions enable you to render more and better service. Wise decisions lead to the production and distribution of more and better goods at lower prices and with a better profit.

Also learn to make only wise decisions concerning your personal and home life. These decisions have much to do with your vocational success and the improvement of your income. One wrong decision at home can wipe out a month's financial progress. Conversely, one very wise decision at home may help you increase your income as much as several weeks of vocational effort.

2. Build The Right Habits And Stop Your Wrong Habits. (Chapters 4 and 5.)

Build the habits which enable you to give more and better service on your job, in your business, or in your profession.

Also eliminate your bad vocational habits. These are the habits which cause you to give less efficient service. If you don't know what these habits are, study a few vocational failures. Or ask your boss, a fellow worker, or a professional consultant.

Give attention to your habits off the job. Sometimes these habits do as much to increase your income as do your efforts while you are actually working. Build the good habits you need and stop your bad habits.

3. *Add To Your Vocational Skills.*

Your vocational skills enable you to give more and better service. In return for the improvement of your skills the community will give you more money.

If you are an executive, for example, develop all the skills of a first-class leader. Develop your skill as a public speaker. Establish a writing skill. Make your letters, announcements, and memoranda read like those of a professional writer.

If you are a salesman, learn everything about your own product and other similar products. Develop skill in the organization of your time. Develop the habit of working hard and long.

If you are a professional man, improve your present vocational skills. Develop new skills which will advance you in your chosen line of work.

Do you perform skilled or semi-skilled work of any kind? Then improve your present skills and add more vocational skills.

4. *Find, Add, Develop, And Learn To Use All The Important Techniques Which Will Advance You In Your Vocation.*

Most of these techniques are of a technical nature. You know them now or you can learn what they are.

5. *Find, Add, Develop, And Learn To Use All The Important Methods.*

You need these methods to help you advance yourself in

your vocation. You also need them to help you get the most out of life.

These methods have to do with getting along well with all sorts of people, with influencing people effectively, with solving problems, achieving goals, thinking straight, thinking positively, and with the development of new, good, and original ideas.

6. Take Excellent Care Of Your Cells. (Chapters 6 and 7.)

Who is going to increase your income? *You! You* are the only one who can improve your services.

In general, the better you care for your cells, the more and better service you can render. The better your cells, the more goods you can produce and distribute at a profit.

A plan has been proposed to increase your income

The plan is to increase your income by the use of six procedures: (1) Make only wise decisions. (2) Build more good new habits which will enable you to give better service in your vocation. Stop old, bad habits which interfere with your efficiency and service. (3) Add to your vocational skills. (4) Become proficient in the use of all the techniques which are important in your vocation. (5) Learn to use all the good methods. (6) Improve the condition of your cells.

It should now be very easy for you to use the Decision-Making Technique. You have all 18 Steps at your finger tips. In any case, look on this as an excellent opportunity to practice.

Use the 18 Steps of the Decision-Making Technique (Chapters 2 and 3). Make your wise decision concerning this First Money Plan.

Is your income too low? Did you, nevertheless, decide against the First Money Plan? Were you unable to find a better plan? Then do whatever is necessary to achieve peace of mind and happiness with an income too small for your needs.

If you decided to accept the plan, simply follow it faithfully. Go a step at a time.

First, follow the Time Plan of Chapter 8. Use your spare time as follows:

Review Chapters 2 and 3. Learn to make only wise decisions.

Then go to work on your vocational habits. Review Chapters 4 and 5. One at a time develop the good vocational habits you need. Eliminate your bad vocational habits.

Next, one after the other, add the vocational skills you need. Learn the vocational techniques you need.

One at a time, learn and use the important methods.

Finally (or first, if you need it most) take excellent care of your cells. Develop more power and energy.

Use all the pertinent suggestions in this book. Increase your income.

You are now, we shall say, using the First Money Plan. You are increasing your earnings.

You don't have to be psychic to see what you must do now. This will give you a hint: Someone said, "There was a time when a fool and his money were soon parted. But now it happens to everybody."

It is now proposed that you live within your income. The proposal is that you spend less than you receive.

That's the proposal. It's very simple. Just pay out less money than you take in.

Do this each month and what happens? You keep some of the money you don't require for your basic needs. Each month, you retain some of your income.

THE SECOND MONEY PLAN—*Spend less than you receive*

The three steps of the Second Money Plan are:

1. *Develop The Right Attitude Toward The Things Money Will Buy.*

Money will buy many of the good things of life. Money will buy power. Money will buy services of all kinds. Money will buy time.

There is nothing wrong with any of these things. They are fine. They're wonderful. But only at the right time and in the right place.

To help yourself spend less than you receive, you should think:

1) "In order to live within my income, I shall look upon everything that costs money as *less desirable.*"

2) "Only those things which are free, or which cost little, are really worth having."

3) "The more something costs the less I shall like it. The less it costs (as long as I get my money's worth) the better I shall like it."

With this thinking well established you will have the right attitude. Then, for example, are you tempted to pay $250 for a suit or dress? Would a $100 or a $50 suit or dress be adequate? If so, you will prefer the lower cost item. Are you tempted to pay $8 for an orchestra seat for a show? Can you see and hear adequately from a $2 seat in the gallery? You will choose the lower-priced seat.

Suppose you consider an evening of commercial entertainment. The other possibility is a pleasant activity with congenial people which costs almost nothing. You will select the inexpensive entertainment.

The right attitude makes it easier for you to follow the plan and live within your income.

2. Get Rid Of The Habit Of Spending Money.

This doesn't mean that you will stop spending money. You will continue to spend most of your income. You will spend it as directed by your wise decisions.

What you are to stop is something else. You are to stop spending money by force of habit. You are to stop the *habit* of spending money.

Turn now to Chapter 5 page 101, *How to Stop a Bad Habit.*

In the fourth step you are directed to the seven Procedures, starting on page 81 of Chapter 4.

First consider Procedure A. How can you avoid or weaken the signals which make you want to spend money?

What are the signals? Many of them are the advertisements which bombard you constantly.

It's easy to avoid many of these signals. Simply skip the commercials if you watch television or listen to the radio. Better still, don't watch TV or listen to the radio except for outstanding programs. Use your time to better advantage.

You can avoid many commercials by passing over the ads in magazines and newspapers without reading them. You can look away and refuse to read the billboards. You can learn to resist salesmen who try to sell you what you shouldn't buy. You can refuse to window-shop.

Now look at Procedures B, C, and D. Weaken your desire to spend money. See to it that your visualized images, inner speech, and implicit muscular movements all have to do (1) with the avoidance of every unnecessary expenditure, (2) with the enjoyment of activities and possessions which cost little, and (3) with holding on to your money.

Use your ingenuity to find the free or very inexpensive entertainment offered by your community. Use your originality to develop ways to get pleasure and satisfaction without spending money. You might get some ideas from the biography of Benjamin Franklin. He developed the habit of frugality.

Refer to Procedure E. Remove or minimize the pleasure that comes with the spending of money. Buy merchandise of good quality, but buy it in plain and not luxurious surroundings. As much as you can, do what buying you must do by yourself. Don't make a party out of it. Don't accompany the spending of money with special treats and rewards, such as hot nut fudge sundaes and fancy lunches.

Now think of Procedure F. Think about the evil consequences of spending money. One bad consequence is that you dissipate your money and you have less for the future. Another is that you may be embarrassed when, later on, you need money and you don't have it.

Finally, there is Procedure G. Happily, there is much you can do to improve your physical condition without spending much money.

All this helps you weaken the *habit* of spending money.

The sixth step under *How to Stop a Bad Habit,* in Chapter 5, directs you back to *How to Establish a Good New Habit,* starting on page 89. You should find it easy to use the suggestions given there in steps 1 to 5. Use them and establish the *habit* of holding on to your money. Establish the *habit* of keeping, as *extra* money, some of the money you receive each month.

3. Practice The Simple Life.

To get an idea of the simple life, think of the Essenes. They lived in Palestine about the time of Christ.

The Essenes despised luxury. Each person had just one white robe.

They all prayed before sunrise. They worked in the fields, vineyards, and orchards from sunrise to sunset. They studied and improved themselves. Their conduct was orderly. The younger people took care of the aged.

The Essenes ate simple, nourishing food. They studied and understood the healing powers of the sun, of fresh air, and of various kinds of baths. They had a special type of positive thinking. There was no illness. They lived to an advanced age.

That was the simple life.

You may not be able to live quite as simply as did the Essenes. But you can visualize their way of living. The visualized pattern will help you practice the simple life.

The simpler you can make your life the less need you will have for money. The less need you have for money the easier will it be to live within your income. *Now use the Decision-Making Technique and make your wise decision.*

If you decided that you will *not* use the Second Money Plan, go right on to the Third Money Plan, below.

Also, if you now spend less than you receive, go on to the next money plan.

If you decided in favor of the plan, look back over the Keys in Chapter 4. Use the Keys to help you follow this Second Money Plan.

Now let us examine the facts in connection with the Third Money Plan.

First Fact. Your *living money* is the money you need (1) for your current expenses, (2) to meet your current financial obligations (debts due and payable, installment payments, and so on), and (3) to meet future obligations including provision for your old age.

Second Fact. Your *extra money* is the money you have left after you spend your living money.

As an example, suppose your net monthly income is $400. You spend $300 every month as living money. Then each month you have $100 of extra money.

Third Fact. Your *leisure money* is money you spend every month for amusement, extra clothes, jewelry, and the entertainment of others. Your leisure money is money you spend primarily for enjoyment.

Fourth Fact. Your *spare money* is the difference between your extra money and your leisure money.

Let's say that you have $100 a month of extra money. You spend $75 a month as leisure money. The difference between the $100 (extra money) and the $75 (leisure money) is $25 (spare money).

Fifth Fact. A good procedure is to deposit your spare money in a savings account. Leave it in the bank or savings institution until you are ready to put it to work.

Sixth Fact. You can make your spare money work *with* you.

One way to make your spare money work with you is to convert it into an education. You can use your spare money to take you through college or through a graduate school. You can use it to pay for special courses and for individual instruction. You can buy books. Then you use the books and education to increase your earnings.

Another way to make your spare money work *with* you is to convert it into special skills or abilities. You do this when you use your spare money to pay for special training courses or for individual instruction. Then you use the skills and earn more money.

You can use some of your spare money to buy whatever you need to take good care of your cells. With an improved physical condition you can earn more.

You make your spare money work with you when you buy special tools, machinery, or equipment which will enable you to provide more and better service.

You make your spare money work with you when you buy a business and you operate it yourself. You do it also when you use your spare money to start your own business.

Seventh Fact. You can make your spare money work *for* you.

Your spare money works *for* you when you put it in a savings account. Your money earns interest.

Your spare money can work for you with other people. Buy an interest in a small business, for example. Then your spare money, in the business, will work for you with the people who operate the business. Your dividends, or share of the profits, is what your money earns.

You can buy stock in a company. Your spare money then works with the company and, you hope, brings you a profit in the form of dividends.

Eighth Fact. When you *speculate,* you buy something with the hope of a greater profit than would come in the ordinary course of business. But with the prospect of greater profit there also comes a greater risk. The larger profit is promised to encourage you to take the additional risk.

If you speculate you realize that you may not get all your money back. You have a chance to make a larger profit. But you also risk the loss of all or part of your money.

Ninth Fact. If you gamble you know you may lose all of the money you risk. It's all in the hands of lady luck. You would not take this big risk without the possibility of an exceptionally large return if you are lucky.

THE THIRD MONEY PLAN—*Handle your spare money wisely*

Here are the eight steps of the Third Money Plan.

1. Set up a simple bookkeeping system. Keep your books by the week or month, according to the way you receive your income. Keep your books so you know exactly what money you receive, what you spend, and how much you have left at the end of each week or month.

2. Make a budget. Budget your money so that each month, in your budget, you have some spare money left after you spend your living money and your leisure money. Try to leave yourself each month, as spare money, 10 percent of your income.

3. Use as many of the Keys and Procedures of Chapter 4 as you need. Make yourself handle your money according to your budget.

4. As soon as you receive your income money, put your spare money in a savings account. There it works for you.

5. Let your spare money pile up in the savings account until you are ready to put it where it will work harder for you.

6. When you are absolutely sure you have a better way of making your spare money work for you, use it according to your selected plan. How can you be sure you have a better plan than the savings account? Use the full Decision-Making Technique and make a wise decision.

7. When you are through using your spare money in a project, put it back in the savings account. Leave it there until you find another better use for it.

8. You may invest your spare money in yourself, as when you pay for additional education. When you do, put at least part of the spare money you earn, as the result of the investment in yourself, back in the savings account with your other spare money.

A Success Story

Here is a success story which illustrates the use of the Third Money Plan.

Sam and Mary had been married for two years. They spent all their income as fast as they received it. Some months they spent more than their income.

One day they learned about the First Money Plan. Sam used the plan. He learned to do his work better. He got a raise.

Then Sam and Mary began to use the Second Money Plan. They found that they could live a lot more economically than had been their habit.

What interested them most was, first, that they enjoyed life just as much as before, and second, that the mutual activity brought them closer together. They were happier.

As the result of their use of the Second Money Plan, Sam and Mary had some spare money every month.

Now they started the Third Money Plan. They discovered that each month they could easily put 10 percent of their income in their savings account.

Sam and Mary continued in this way for five years. They watched their spare money grow to $3700.

Then, one day, out of a clear sky, Sam's boss asked him if he would like to come into the business with him as his partner.

Sam and Mary immediately used the Decision-Making Technique. Sam already knew all about the business. He had all the general facts. The boss had outlined the plan. The most important fact was that it would require a $3,000 investment.

Sam and Mary decided in favor of the plan. They realized that it was a wonderful opportunity.

Sam and Mary were both especially happy because they had the needed cash.

As a partner, Sam's income doubled. But Sam and Mary continued with the Third Money Plan. They put 10 percent of their net income into the savings account as spare money.

In ten years Sam's partner died. Sam bought his interest from the estate.

Sam continued to use the First Money Plan. Under Sam's direction the business prospered even more than before. Soon the demand forced Sam to establish branches in other cities.

Sam and Mary are rich and happy.

Would You Prefer A Different Story?

You can easily write a story of your own.

Simply search your memory for the plot. You may know of many instances where someone considered a franchise, a small business, or a part interest in a business. He used the Decision-Making Technique and he made a wise selection. Then he used the three Money Plans. When he had enough spare money he bought the franchise or the business. Then, because he used the First Money Plan, the business prospered.

Or you may know of someone who simply saved his money on general principles. Then the opportunity he had been waiting for presented itself. He had the necessary cash and he was able to seize the opportunity.

Specifically, you might know about the couple who had saved $3500 which, they thought, would be enough to start a certain type of hamburger place. They started their business venture. It was successful. Now they have seven Hamburger Hamlets and their annual gross is $5,000,000.

Possibly you heard of the man who had saved $3800. He had no project in mind, but he felt that something would appear. One day, and very unexpectedly, he was offered a very lucrative franchise. It needed $3500 cash. The man bought the franchise and, during the course of the next fifteen years, he paid income taxes on a total personal income of over $2,000,000.

Many a person has had an idea. He used the three Money Plans. He put his money with his idea and became a millionaire.

Use the Decision-Making Technique and make your decision.

Will you follow this Third Money Plan? Will you reject it? Be sure to use all 18 Steps.

Did you decide not to use this Third Money Plan? Then go on with the reading.

Did you decide to accept the Third Money Plan? Then follow it. Continue with the Third Money Plan until, with an assist from the other two money plans, you have all the money you want.

Chapter 10

THE GOLDEN SECRET

*In this short chapter you learn the one
Golden Secret. Use it. Get what you
want from life.*

The magic secret

Many plans and suggestions are offered in this book. Of all of them there is one which stands far above all the rest. This is the one Magic Secret which brings you the good things of life. It is the Magic Secret which helps you most on your trip into the future. Without it all the other plans and suggestions may be as nothing.

Can you see which part of which plan is the Magic Secret?

It is steps C and D of the Time Plan, in Chapter 8.

First, the Magic Secret is your ability to find plenty of spare time. Second, it is your ability to look upon each minute of your spare time as a minute of opportunity and to use each minute to get more power.

When you have enough power, the Magic Secret is your ability to look upon every minute of your spare time as an opportunity and to use your spare time to get the good things of life.

How many plans did you accept?

It is presumed that, as you read this book, you made your decision, one way or the other, for each plan suggested.

Almost surely you accepted some of the plans. You may be using one or more of the plans right now. In this way you are bringing more good things into your life.

If this is true, all you have to do is continue. Use your spare time. Follow the plans you have selected. Add other plans as seems advisable. Continue until you have all the good things you want.

On the other hand, you may have decided in favor of *all* the plans. If you did, here is a suggestion. Select the plan which you think should be mastered first. Then use your spare time and establish the use of the selected plan as a habit. This may require a month. It may take six months. In any case, continue with the first selected plan until its use is habitual.

Then, one after the other, begin the use of the other plans suggested in this book. One at a time establish them as habits.

This may take five years. It may require ten. But who cares? You don't care if it takes all the rest of your life, because every day—*you enjoy more of the good things of life!*

As you journey through life

What happens when your cells are in excellent condition and you are always well and strong? When you get along well with everyone at home? When you are popular with the people around you? When your education is adequate? When you adjust easily to members of the opposite sex? When you have a good sexual adjustment? When you are comfortable with your religious beliefs? When you are happy in your work and vocationally successful? When you have a happy marriage? When you are calm and emotionally stable? When you think clearly and logically? And when you have plenty of money which you handle wisely?

What happens when, as you travel through life, you have a good adjustment in each of the twelve fields? This is what happens—

Life emits "a fragrance like flowers and sweet-smelling herbs."

You greet each day with joy!

A hundred times a day you are glad you were born!

Bon voyage!

INDEX